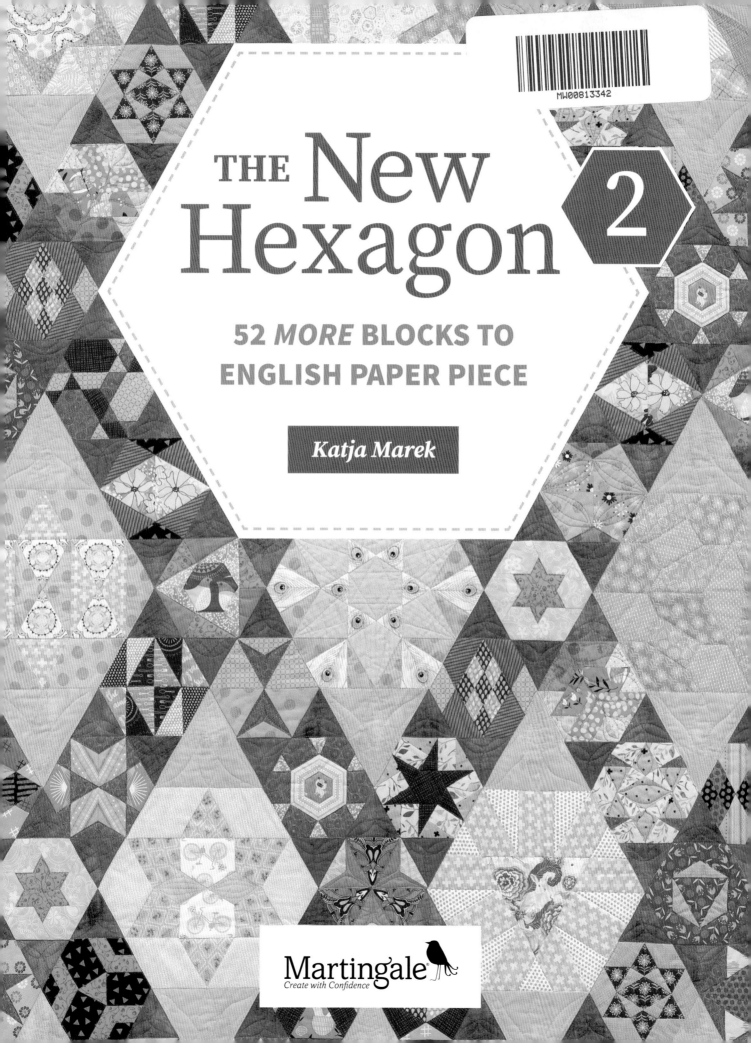

THE New Hexagon 2

52 *MORE* BLOCKS TO ENGLISH PAPER PIECE

Katja Marek

Martingale®
Create with Confidence

The New Hexagon 2: 52 *More* Blocks to English Paper Piece
© 2019 by Katja Marek

Martingale®
19021 120th Ave. NE, Ste. 102
Bothell, WA 98011-9511 USA
ShopMartingale.com

Printed in China
24 23 22 21 20 19   8 7 6 5 4 3 2 1

Library of Congress Control Number: 2019941962

ISBN: 978-1-68356-036-4

MISSION STATEMENT

We empower makers who use fabric and yarn to make life more enjoyable.

CREDITS

PUBLISHER AND
CHIEF VISIONARY OFFICER
Jennifer Erbe Keltner

CONTENT DIRECTOR
Karen Costello Soltys

DESIGN MANAGER
Adrienne Smitke

MANAGING EDITOR
Tina Cook

PRODUCTION MANAGER
Regina Girard

ACQUISITIONS AND
DEVELOPMENT EDITOR
Laurie Baker

COVER AND
BOOK DESIGNER
Kathy Kotomaimoce

TECHNICAL EDITOR
Nancy Mahoney

PHOTOGRAPHER
Brent Kane

COPY EDITOR
Marcy Heffernan

ILLUSTRATORS
Sandy Loi
Linda Schmidt

SPECIAL THANKS

Cover photography for this book was taken at Blackberry Hill Farm in Carnation, Washington.

DEDICATION

For my sister Sabine, who I lost so long ago. Even back then we shared a love for crafting and sewing. I hope that she'd be proud of me.

To my customers, followers, and fellow quilters who have embraced my designs and by so doing have fueled my desire to do more. And to my ever-supportive staff, who by pitching in when I come up with something new, allow me to do what I love.

You have all been such an important part of my journey, because without even one of you, the journey would not have been the same.

Contents

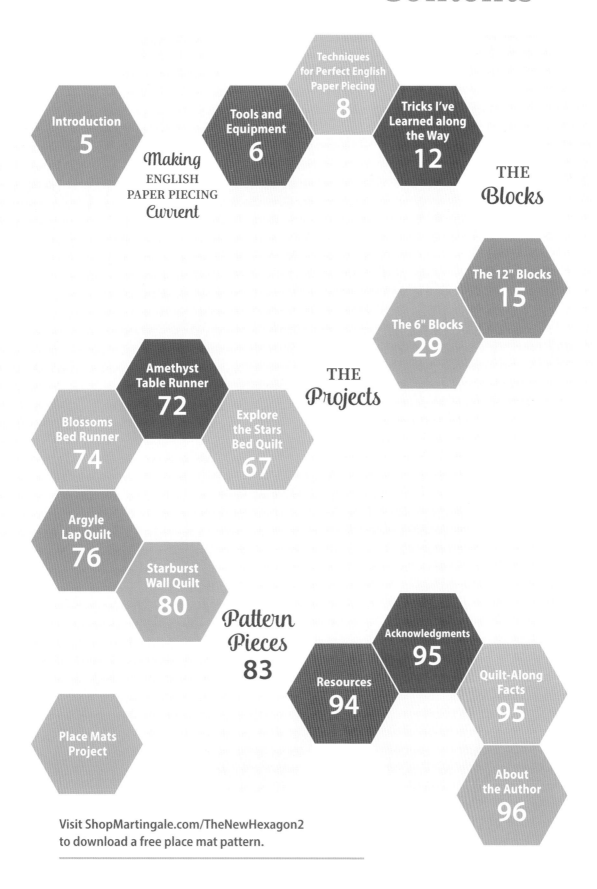

Visit ShopMartingale.com/TheNewHexagon2
to download a free place mat pattern.

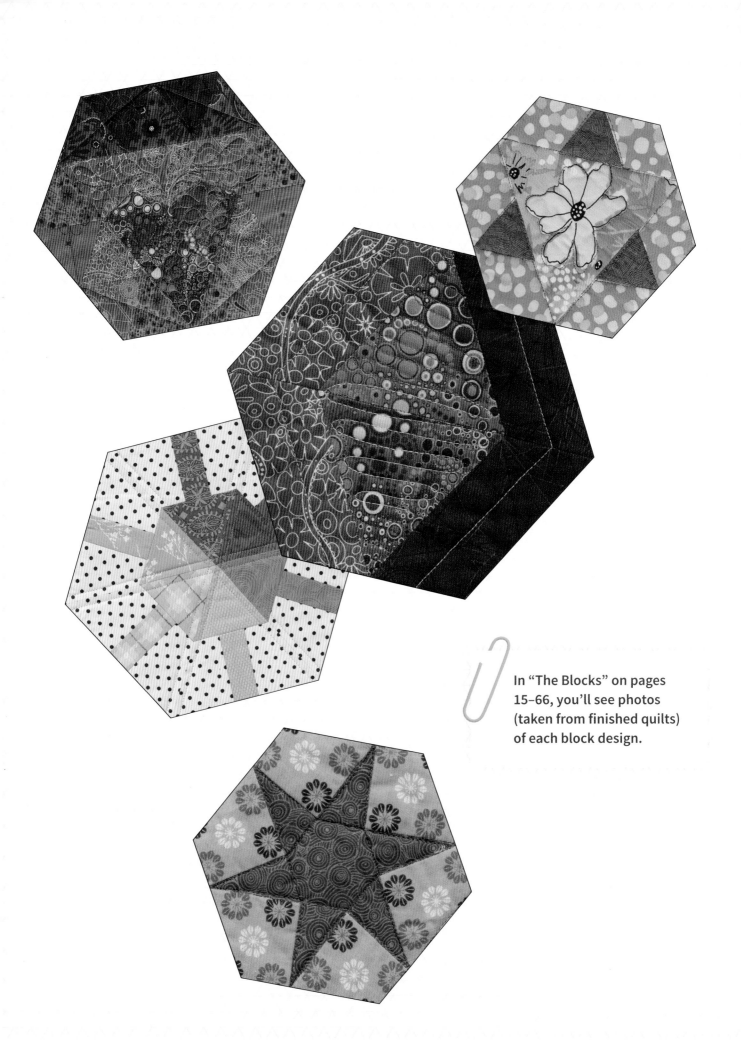

In "The Blocks" on pages 15–66, you'll see photos (taken from finished quilts) of each block design.

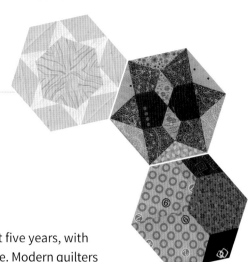

Introduction

English paper piecing has seen a huge resurgence in the last five years, with creative new shape combinations to tempt our quilting palate. Modern quilters are adopting this wonderfully portable technique as though they themselves—instead of pioneering women several hundred years before us—had invented it. Paper piecing is a technique that has been brought into this century with new tools and techniques, such as fabric glue for basting, die-cut paper shapes to baste around, and laser-cut acrylics to fussy cut our fabrics.

When I designed the blocks for *The New Hexagon: 52 Blocks to English Paper Piece* (Martingale, 2014) and *The New Hexagon Perpetual Calendar* (Martingale, 2016), the ideas just didn't seem to stop. My database of fractured hexagon blocks grew and grew. So when Martingale asked me to put together some ideas for *The New Hexagon 2,* I was pretty excited!

But this time, we agreed that we wanted more than one size of block. So for this book I've designed 52 brand-new blocks: 14 blocks that are 12" hexagons, and 38 blocks that are 6" hexagons. It was a fun challenge to find creative ways to combine the two different-sized blocks in projects.

After *The New Hexagon* was published, many people asked me about the names of the blocks. My first book began as an in-house block-a-week program in my shop, which far surpassed my expectations. When Martingale accepted my book proposal based on those blocks, I decided to name the blocks after 52 of the women who were the most faithful to the program and in turn helped to make it so successful.

With this book and 52 new blocks, I've decided to name the blocks for women I admire both in the quilting industry and in my life. I hope that you too will find a connection through these blocks and projects.

Still discovering the hex-abilities!

~Katja

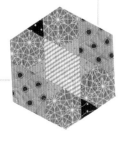

Making English Paper Piecing Current

Change is inevitable. English paper piecing is a good example of this. As products and techniques evolve, quilters find new ways to streamline once-laborious techniques to suit their lifestyles. On the pages that follow, you'll find my favorite techniques, tips, and tricks to translate blocks into quilts more quickly than before.

Tools and Equipment

Choosing the correct tools can make the quiltmaking process much easier. The following are products that I've used successfully for my English paper piecing. For more information about where to find many of the tools listed, see "Resources" on page 94.

Paper

I use 67-pound cover stock paper to print my own patterns, because it's the ideal weight for English paper piecing. I've found that it's flexible enough to bend at intersecting seams and sturdy enough to give a nice sharp edge for glue basting. As an alternative, precut papers for English paper piecing are available from Paper Pieces.

Laser-Cut Acrylic Templates

The easiest way to cut fabric pieces accurately (which is a must for English paper piecing), as well as fussy cut fabrics for kaleidoscope effects, is to use precision laser-cut acrylic templates. I've worked with Paper Pieces to create acrylic templates for the patterns in this book, as well as those in my previous publications, to streamline this technique.

Marking Tools

I use a Collins Fine Line Water Erasable Marking Pen for all fabrics, except the darkest ones. For dark fabrics, I use a Clover white marking pen. The markings from both pens can be removed with water. I also use a Hera marker, a spatula-like gadget, which makes visible indentations in the fabric. Simply run it along the edge of a ruler when marking simple straight lines.

Basting Glue

I've often been heard to say that glue revolutionized my life. I prefer glue to thread basting, because it saves time and streamlines the process. I use a Fons & Porter water-soluble fabric glue stick. This refillable stick has a surface area that is slightly more than ¼" diameter, much smaller than a traditional glue stick, making it perfect for glue basting seam allowances. The glue goes on blue and dries clear, so you can see where it has been applied and if you have sufficient coverage. Most importantly, the glue stick is designed for use on fabric, ensuring that you'll be able to remove the papers when needed. (Not all glue sticks work this way!)

Add-Three-Eighths Ruler

Using the Add-Three-Eighths Ruler from CM Designs and a rotary cutter is the easiest way to achieve consistently accurate seam allowances when cutting out your fabrics. The ⅜" lip on the underside of the ruler can easily be aligned along the edge of the paper template, ensuring precise results every time.

Needles

I use Clover Black Gold appliqué needles in size 10 for hand sewing. I was given these needles as a sample to try, and I find they stand up to my usual tendency to bend or snap needles. They are extremely sharp and glide through the fabric with ease.

Thread

There is great division over what type of thread to use both for hand sewing and for machine sewing. Since writing *The New Hexagon,* I've been asked to test various threads and have found a few favorites: Mettler Silk Finish 50-weight 100% cotton thread, Aurifil 50-weight 100% cotton thread available in a fabulous selection of colors, Superior Masterpiece cotton thread, which comes on prewound bobbins in a selection of 35 colors contained in a handy bobbin storage ring, and InvisaFil 100-weight 2-ply cottonized polyester that is so thin yet strong that it sinks in and becomes virtually invisible.

Although there's an unwritten "rule" that you should never use a polyester thread to sew cotton fabric, I firmly believe that advances in technology and the quality of the threads available to us today have disproved this belief. I use a coordinating thread color to whipstitch the pieces together to make the hexagon blocks. When appliquéing the blocks to a background fabric, I match the thread color to the fabric of the block being appliquéd.

Needle Threader

Having a needle threader handy can make many a sewing job easier. I've come to that point in my life where I can't seem to do without one. Although I use the Clover desktop needle threader, you may find that any traditional simple needle threader will work for you.

Binder Clips

Binder clips are used to hold sheets of paper together. They come in many sizes; I use small ¾" clips to hold the edges of the pieces together so they don't shift when I'm whipstitching. Since I can fold the little handles down, there is nothing to get in the way and impede my stitching.

Reading Glasses (Magnifiers)

I've worn glasses most of my life, and switched to progressive lenses over 15 years ago, but sometimes I feel like I can't see things big enough. My optometrist said he could make me a pair of sewing glasses, but then I wouldn't be able to watch TV while sewing. I do much of my English paper piecing in the evening in front of the TV. My solution was to wear reading glasses over my progressive lenses to magnify the area I needed to see while piecing. My optometrist said this was a workable solution that would not affect my eyesight detrimentally. So if you need to see things "bigger," try magnifiers or reading glasses to make the job less strenuous.

Tailor's Awl

I find that a straight tailor's awl is the most effective tool for removing glue-basted papers. It slides easily between the seam allowance and the paper template to loosen the glue.

Best Press

Before I remove the paper templates from pieces that will be appliquéd to a background, I use a pressing agent, such as Mary Ellen's Best Press. It's an alternative to starch and sizing that gives a nice sharp edge to my work and allows it to maintain its shape even after the papers have been removed.

Appliqué Pins

Appliqué pins are short (usually about ¾" long) and used to hold appliqué shapes in position on background or other fabric pieces. The advantage of these little pins over regular pins is that there is less pin for the thread to tangle around. With long pins, the thread often gets caught on the head or point, which can be very frustrating. I prefer pins with a rounded head, such as Clover appliqué pins, which leave even less chance of tangling while appliquéing.

On-the-Go Box

I like to have a container handy and ready to go with all the supplies I need for English paper piecing. You can use any plastic container with a lid that fits firmly. It should be about 9" x 12" and 2" to 3" high. Your on-the-go box should contain all the essentials, including small paper scissors, small sharp fabric scissors, needles, needle threader, thread, binder clips, marking tools, glue stick and refills, paper for making patterns or die-cut paper shapes for the project you're making, and a small selection of fabrics for piecing.

Basting Spray

I don't have the time or inclination to spend hours thread or pin basting quilt layers prior to quilting, but I have discovered that using 505 Temporary Fabric Adhesive is a great solution. I save time and don't have to deal with the unsightly holes that safety pins have occasionally left in my quilts, especially when I have been working with tightly woven fabrics like batiks. Make sure to use basting spray in a well ventilated area.

Techniques for Perfect English Paper Piecing

Since my first book, *The New Hexagon,* was released in October 2014, the popularity of English paper piecing has grown by leaps and bounds. Quilters have discovered just how portable this technique is, and how a few minutes here and there can add up to completed projects in no time at all.

Preparing Paper Templates

1. Choose the number of blocks required for your project from "The 12" Blocks" (pages 15–28) or "The 6" Blocks" (pages 29–66).

2. Referring to "Pattern Pieces" on pages 83–93, photocopy the required number of patterns for the chosen block onto cover stock.

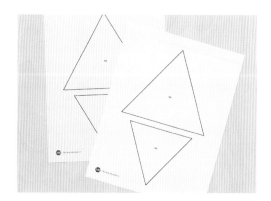

3. To make templates, cut out each photocopied pattern on the printed lines, trimming away and discarding the excess paper. Cut through the center of the lines (as opposed to cutting outside the lines or cutting off the lines completely) to achieve the most accurate piecing.

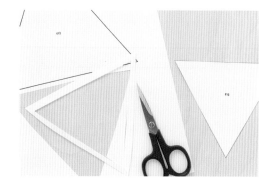

Die-Cut Paper Pieces

These instructions show how to make your own papers pieces and how to use them. If you'd prefer to skip the first part of the process, you can purchase die-cut paper pieces to make each of the blocks in this book. Look for "The New Hexagon 2: Complete Block Piecing Pack" at your local quilt shop or online at PaperPieces.com.

The die-cut templates are not labeled, so before using them be sure to label each piece with its letter and number, referring to the patterns on pages 83–93. First sort by shape using the list on page 83 as a guide, then sort the pieces in each group by size.

4. Pay extra attention to any templates that need to be reversed. Mark the template letter and number on the unmarked side of the paper template.

5. Cut all the required template papers for the chosen block. Lay out the paper templates as the block will be pieced, with the marked letter/number facing up.

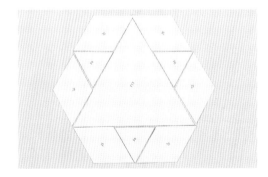

Basting the Individual Pieces

To ensure the directional blocks match the orientation of the blocks shown in this book, lay out the block templates as shown in the block diagram. Always glue the top or marked side of the paper template to the *wrong* side of the fabric.

1. Lay out the paper templates to look like the printed block you're making. Using a glue stick, apply a few lines of glue on the top (numbered side) of the paper template.

2. Flip the template over, positioning it onto the wrong side of your chosen fabric. Glue basting the template to the fabric allows for greater precision with fussy cutting, since you can accurately place the paper template on the desired design element on your fabric. For more details, see "Fussy Cutting for Kaleidoscope Effects" on page 14.

3. Cut out the fabric shape, adding ⅜" seam allowance all around the paper template. Use a rotary-cutting ruler extended ⅜" beyond the edge of the template *OR,* use the Add-Three-Eighths ruler as shown. This specialty ruler has a ⅜"-wide lip that makes aligning it a breeze.

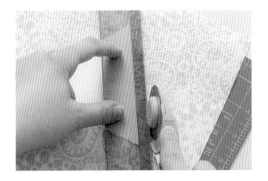

4. Apply a line of glue on the template *near* the edge of the paper. Stay away from the actual edge, since trying to whipstitch through the glue can be difficult. Add a dab of glue to the fabric along each end of the paper for more accurate basting.

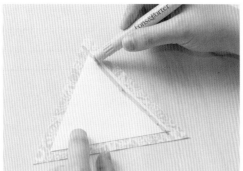

Seam Allowance

TIP

Experience has taught me that a ⅜" seam allowance is preferable to ¼". The slightly larger allowance means that if your paper template shifts a little off center, you won't end up with a too-short seam allowance on one side, which can leave your seams vulnerable to fraying.

5. Finger-press the seam allowance onto the glue line and hold momentarily to secure.

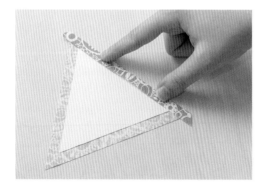

6. Continue in the same way until all the seam allowances are glue basted to the template. Notice that the tails of fabric at the ends of the template are left free, sticking out beyond the edge of the paper template, and not folded back or glued.

7. Glue baste all of the pieces for the block you're making. Lay out the pieces using the original block diagram.

Joining Pieces into a Block

1. Thread your needle and tie a knot in one end of the thread. Do not use a double strand.

2. On the paper side of the piece, insert the needle under the seam allowance, bringing the needle out at the corner and hiding the knot under the fabric.

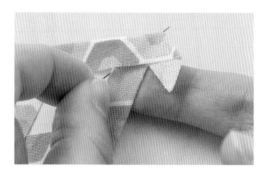

3. Hold two adjoining glue-basted pieces right sides together, aligning the edges to be joined and matching the corner points. Whipstitch along the folded edges, making sure the needle enters the fabric perpendicular to the fabric edge. The thread will angle across the folded edges, but very little thread will show on the finished side of your block. Take care to catch only one or two threads of fabric along the fold, using small stitches (about 12 stitches per inch). Do not stitch through the paper.

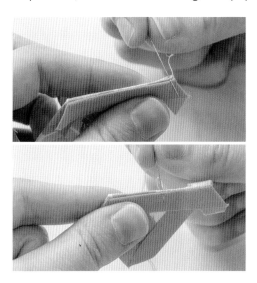

4. Secure the end of the stitching line with several locking backstitches as follows. At the end of the seam, place the needle through the fabric as though to take a stitch backward, about 1/8" to the right of from the last stitch. Run the thread behind the back (eye end) of the needle, up, over, and across the needle, and loop the thread around the tip of the needle. Pull the thread snugly to the needle before pulling the thread through to complete the stitch.

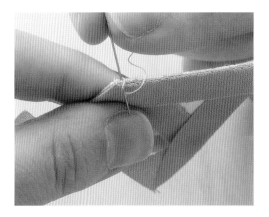

5. When the end of one seam leads directly to another, secure the thread as in step 4 (below left), but do not cut it. Continue without tying off between seams, sewing until no more pieces can be added, and then tie off with the locking backstitch and cut the thread.

6. Whipstitch all the seams to complete the block. Tie off with several locking backstitches.

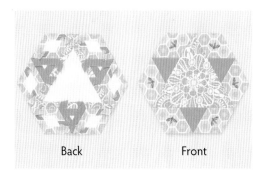

Back   Front

Inset Seams

When inserting a piece that requires an inset or Y seam, whipstitch the first arm of the Y. At the end of seam 1, make one locking backstitch. Instead of tying off the thread, fold the paper templates to align the next seam. Start with a locking backstitch, and then whipstitch to the end. Tie off with several locking backstitches.

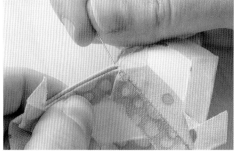

Removing Basting Papers

When the outer edges of a basted piece are completely surrounded by other pieces and all the seams are whipstitched closed, it's time to remove the paper template. Simply slide the tip of a tailor's awl under the fabric edge, between the fabric and the paper template, to loosen the edge. Then gently remove the papers.

What to Do with the Fabric Tails

TIP

I try to glue my seam allowances working in the same direction, either clockwise or counterclockwise. This way when I have groups of similar shapes coming together, the tails will flow neatly.

With these hexagon blocks many different shapes are being joined, and it's almost impossible to predict how the tails will nest between different shapes. So you'll have to fold them out of the way, whipstitch the seam, and then let the tail fall back into place.

One thing you should *never* do is cut off the tails or try to fold them inward on sharp points like triangles, diamonds, half-hexagons, or any shape with a point that's less than 90°.

Tricks I've Learned along the Way

During my years of quilting, crafting, and stitching, I've discovered many little tricks and tips that I think you'll find immensely helpful.

Why Pieces Don't Fit

I'm often asked, "Why don't the pieces fit after adding the fabric?" When you stop to think about it, it makes sense. We cut a paper block into its individual pieces. After cutting, the pieces fit perfectly, and then we add a layer of fabric at each cut edge and still expect the pieces to fit perfectly, even though there is extra bulk at every seam. Notice that the edges line up, even though there are no divisions on one side of the long seam and two divisions on the other side.

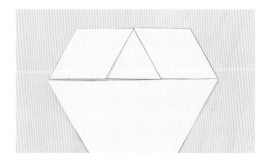

Once the fabric is added around each piece, the top section is longer than the bottom piece and the ends no longer line up.

To make the pieces fit together correctly, line up the starting corner and whipstitch the first bit of the seam, then insert a locking backstitch to hold everything in place. Line up the ending corners and use binder clips to hold the pieces in place while sewing. Ease in the middle by curving the edges against your fingers and finish whipstitching the seam. Have faith: if you line up each end of the seam and ease in the middle, the pieces will fit beautifully once the papers are removed. Remember, fabric is more flexible than paper!

Accurately Glue-Basted Templates

The results of your English paper piecing will be determined in large part by the accuracy of your glue basting. Refer to steps 1–4 of "Basting the Individual Pieces" on page 9 to glue baste the pieces, making sure to place a dab of glue on the fabric along each end of the paper template for more accurate basting. That way when the subsequent seam allowance is glued down, the first seam allowance can't open up inadvertently at the corner. It also ensures that each corner will be as accurate as the paper template. Accurately glued corners and angles can help you to match up glue-basted pieces.

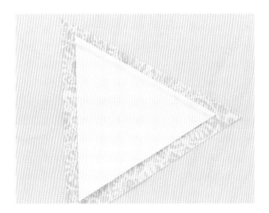

Soft Glue

In warmer weather a glue stick can become a little soft, making it difficult to apply the correct amount of glue. Simply pop the glue stick into the refrigerator for a few minutes to let it harden a bit, and then proceed as usual.

Use the Tails to Align the Pieces

If you make sure to always glue the corners tightly with accurate angles, you can use the line of the tails extending beyond the pieces to line up the piece next to it. I sometimes line up the two adjacent pieces on a flat surface, press down onto one piece where the tail is underlying it to make sure it doesn't shift, and then fold the second piece onto the first, using the tail to keep everything lined up.

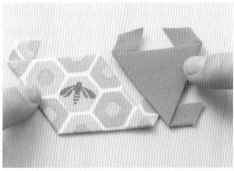

Fussy Cutting for Kaleidoscope Effects

Fussy cutting fabrics can create stunning kaleidoscope effects in these blocks. To fussy cut, identify a repeating design element on your fabric and place your paper template on the desired design, applying a small line of glue to the template to prevent shifting. Be sure to place the three or six pieces over the identical design element on your fabric to create a kaleidoscope effect. A bit of subtle fussy cutting was done for some of the blocks in "Explore the Stars" on page 67, as well as "Argyle" on page 76.

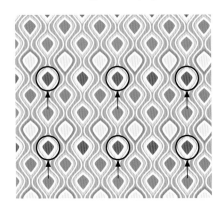

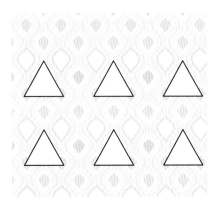

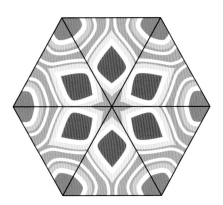

Block Sizes

Since a hexagon is made up of equilateral triangles, the size of a block is determined by measuring the outside edge of the hexagon and doubling that number. For the 12" blocks, the side of the hexagon is 6" (6" x 2 = 12"). For the 6" blocks, the side of the hexagon is 3" (3" x 2 = 6").

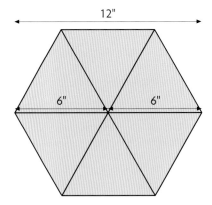

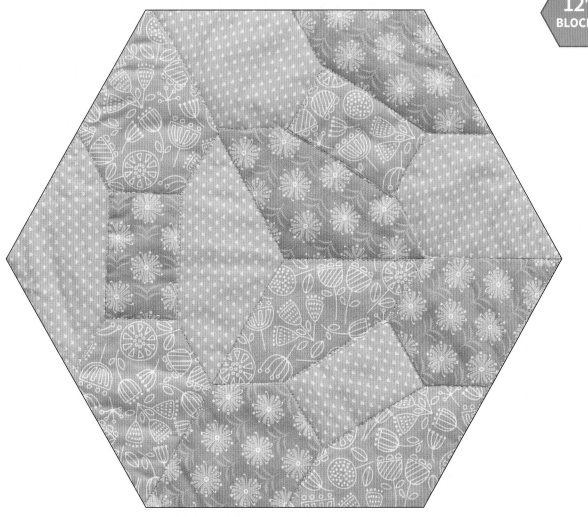

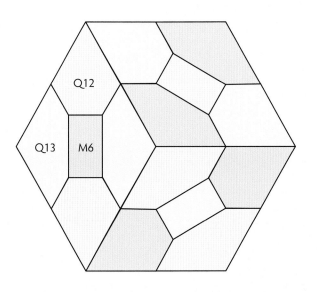

What to Cut

- 3 of M6
- 6 *each* of Q12 and Q13

Carrie

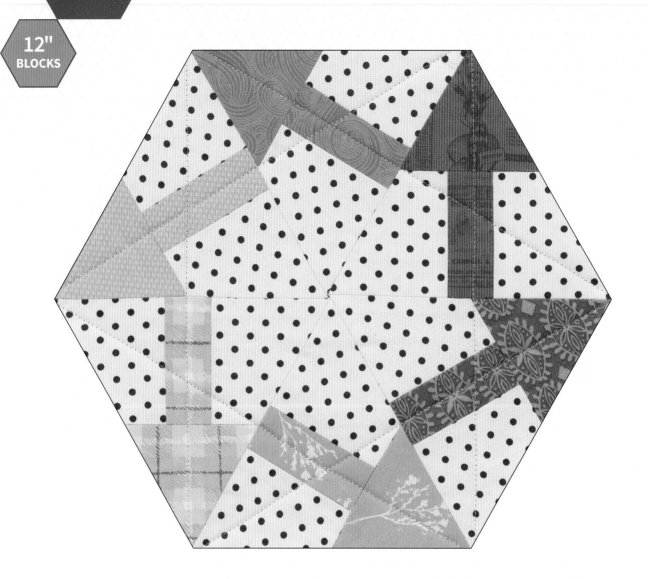

What to Cut

- 6 *each* of E3, E3 reversed, F10, and M7

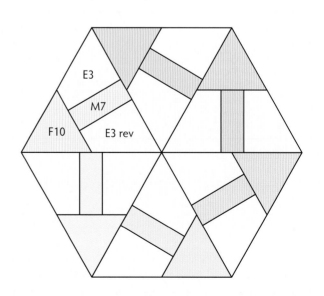

BLOCK
3

12"
BLOCKS

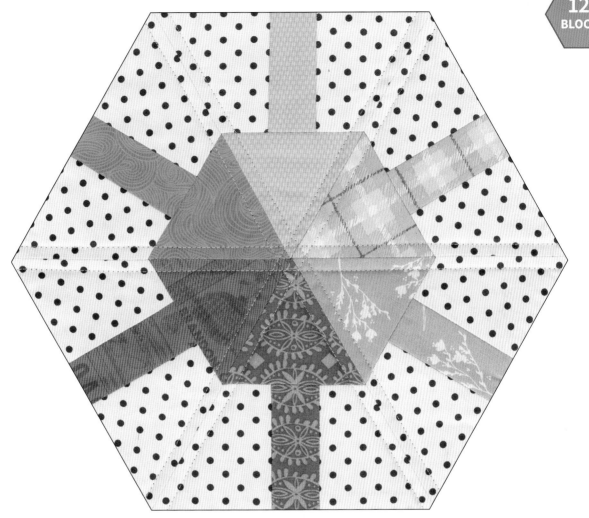

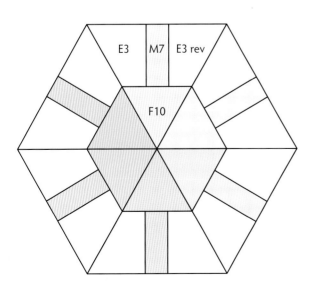

| E3 | M7 | E3 rev |

F10

What to Cut

- 6 *each* of E3, E3 reversed, F10, and M7

Kim

What to Cut

- 6 *each* of C4, F8, F11, and P2
- 12 of K5

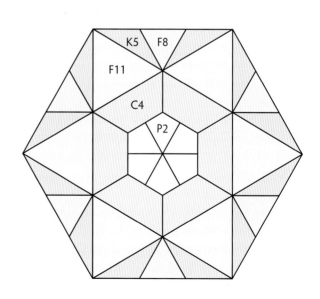

Alison

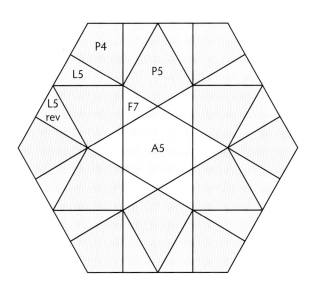

What to Cut

- 1 of A5
- 6 *each* of F7, L5, L5 reversed, P4, and P5

Aileen

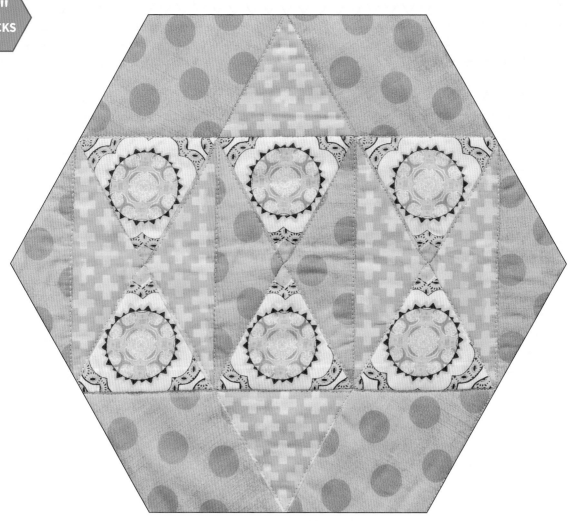

What to Cut

- 4 of J9
- 8 *each* of F10 and K4

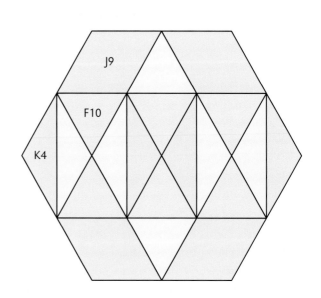

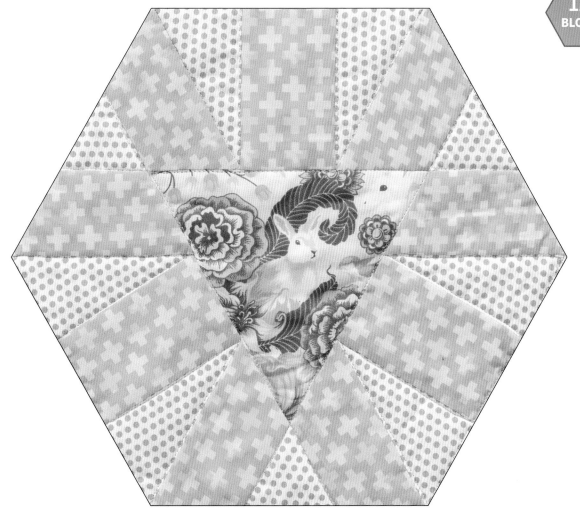

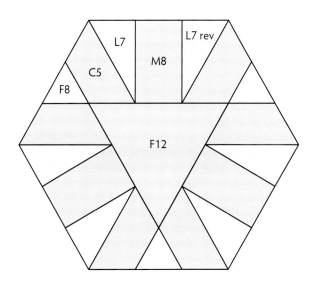

What to Cut

- 1 of F12
- 3 *each* of F8, L7, L7 reversed, and M8
- 6 of C5

Brigitte

What to Cut

- 6 of P5
- 12 *each* of F10 and K3

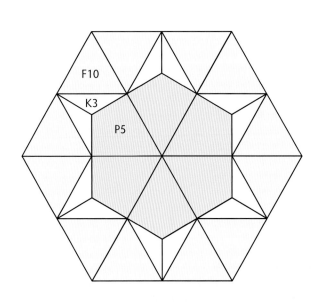

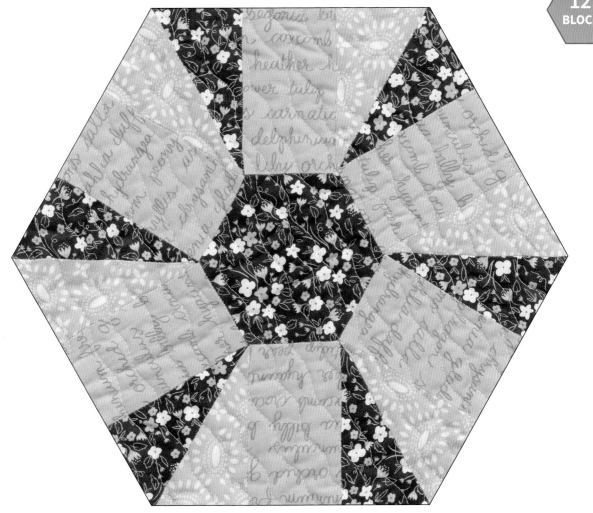

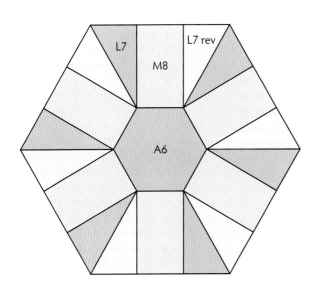

What to Cut

- 1 of A6
- 6 *each* of L7, L7 reversed, and M8

Sheryl

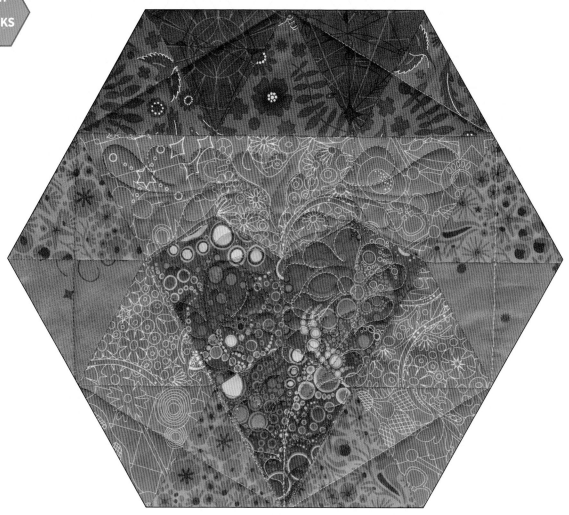

What to Cut

- 3 *each* of P5 and Q14
- 15 of F10

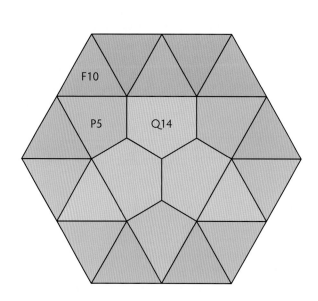

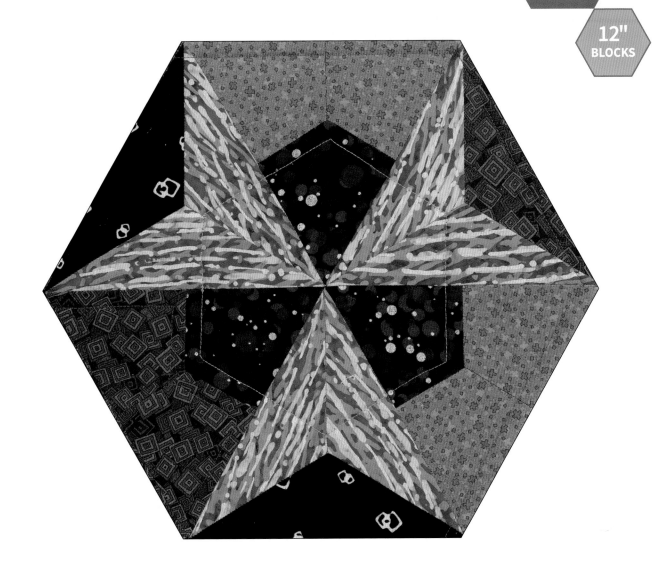

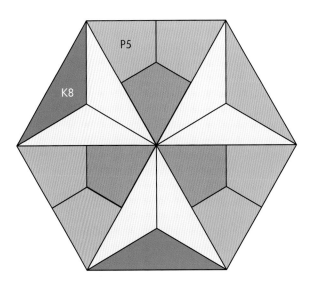

What to Cut

- 9 *each* of K8 and P5

Rebecca

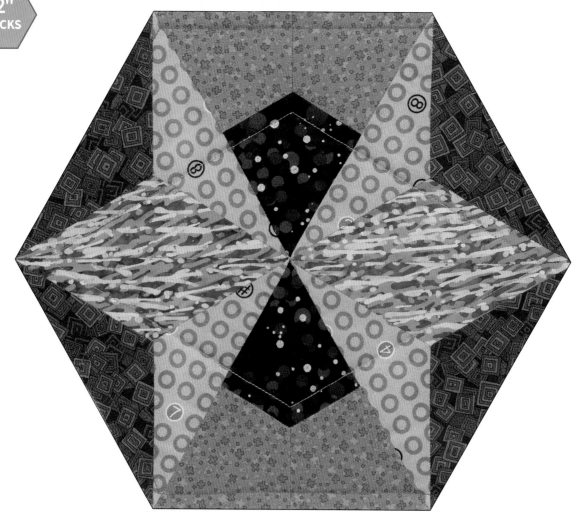

What to Cut

- 6 of P5
- 12 of K8

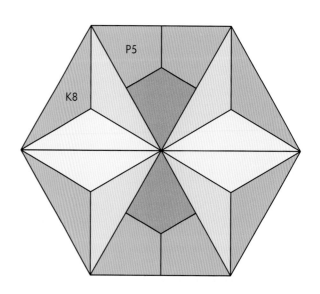

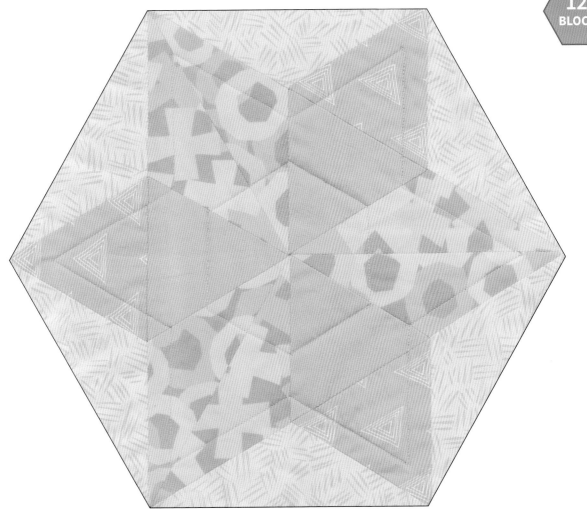

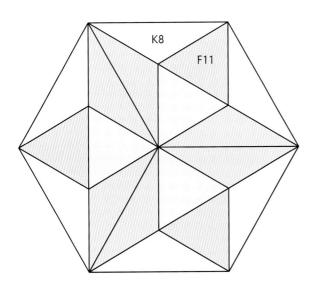

What to Cut

- 6 of F11
- 12 of K8

Karen

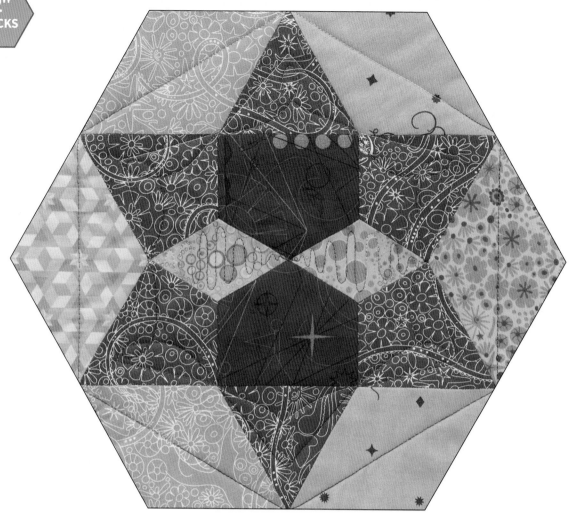

What to Cut

- 2 *each* of F10, J6, and Q14
- 4 of P5
- 6 of J9

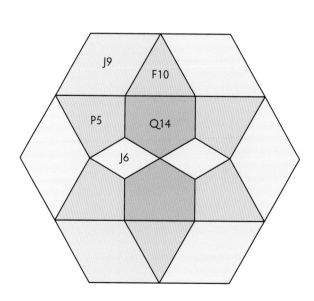

Melissa

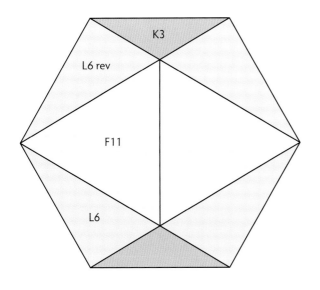

What to Cut

- 2 *each* of F11, K3, L6, and L6 reversed

Veronica

What to Cut

- 6 of F4
- 12 *each* of F7 and K1

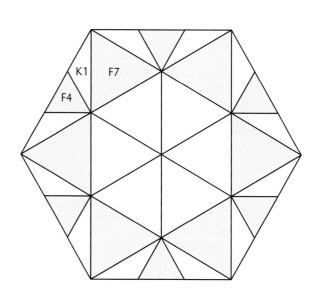

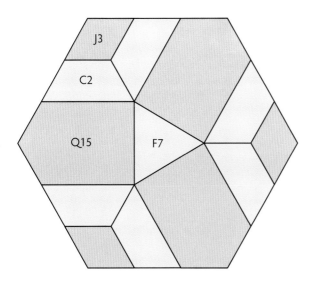

What to Cut

- 1 of F7
- 3 *each* of J3 and Q15
- 6 of C2

Lynette

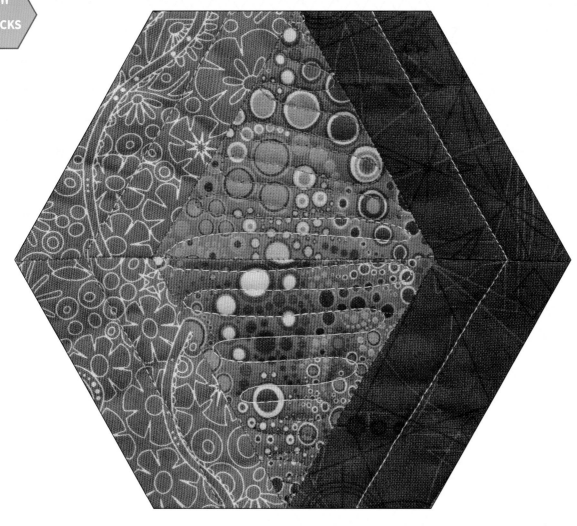

What to Cut

- 2 *each* of F10, N4, and N4 reversed

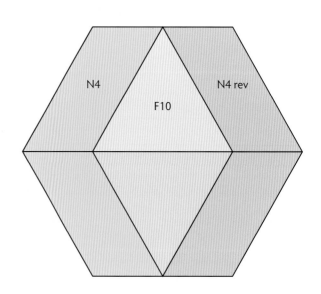

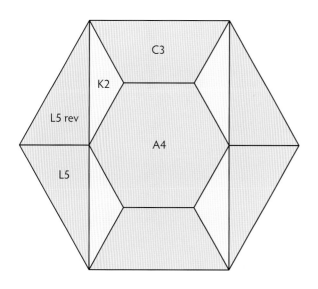

What to Cut

- 1 of A4
- 2 *each* of C3, L5, and L5 reversed
- 4 of K2

April

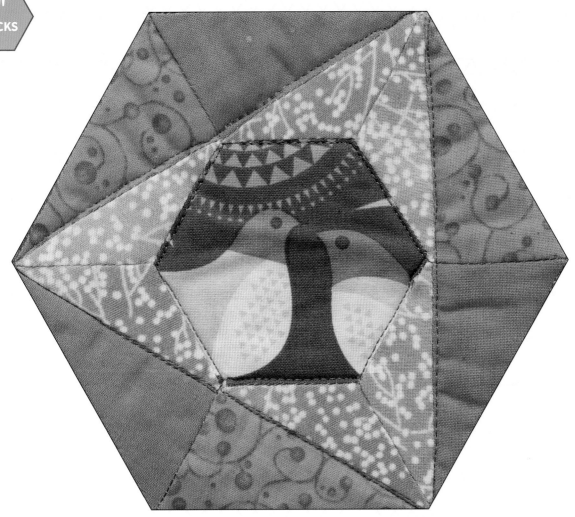

What to Cut

- 1 of A4
- 3 *each* of L5 and L5 reversed
- 6 of K2

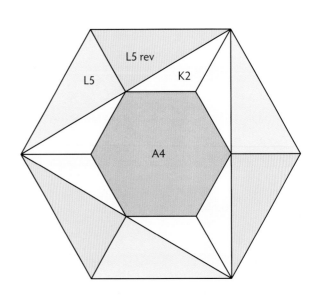

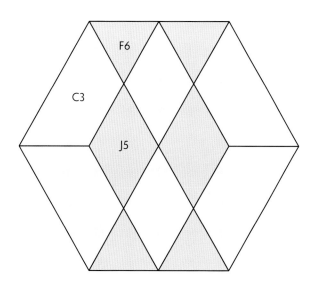

What to Cut

- 4 *each* of C3, F6, and J5

Amy

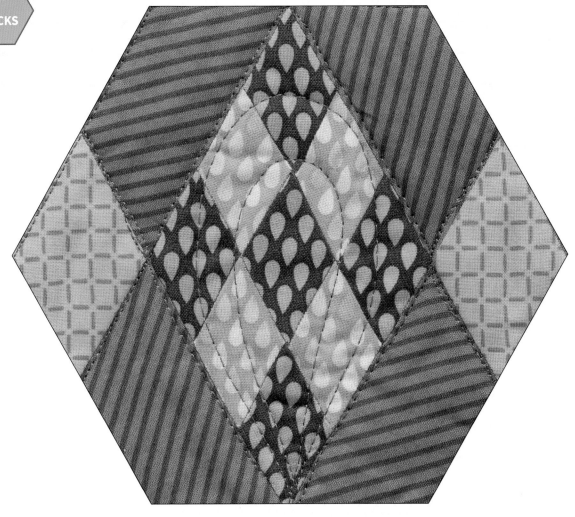

What to Cut

- 2 of J5
- 4 of C3
- 9 of J3

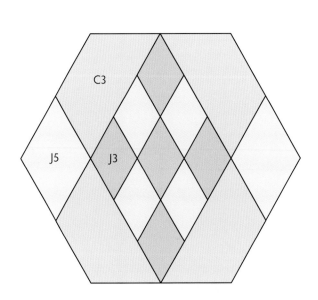

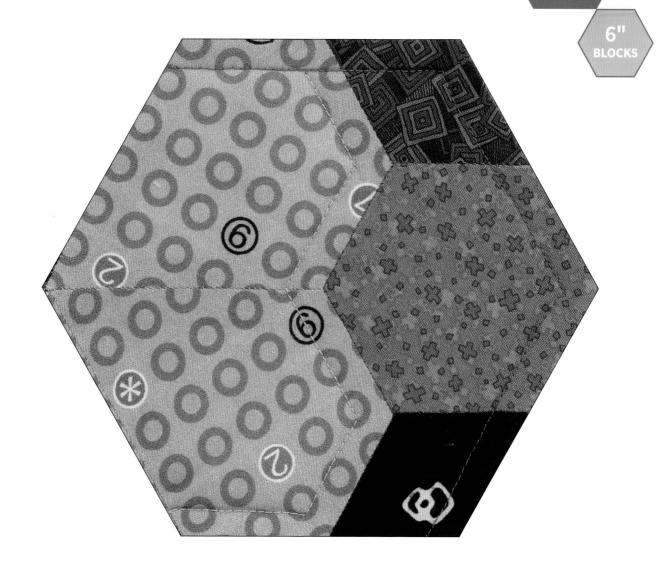

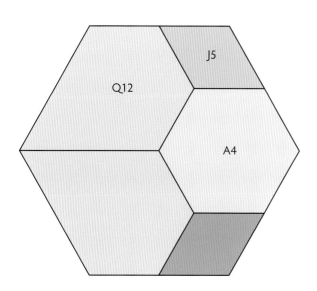

What to Cut

- 1 of A4
- 2 *each* of J5 and Q12

Pat

What to Cut

• 6 *each* of E1, E1 reversed, and K2

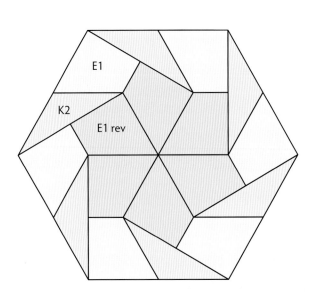

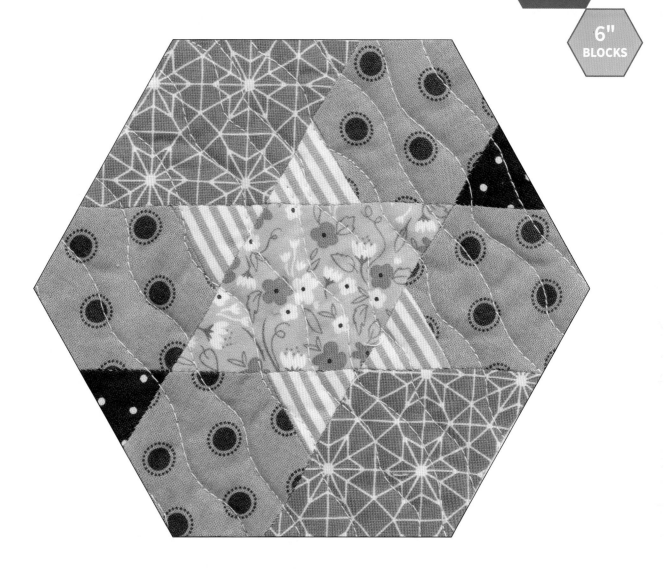

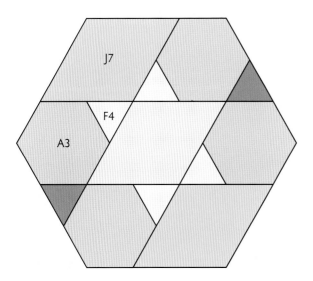

What to Cut

- 3 of J7
- 4 of A3
- 6 of F4

Michelle

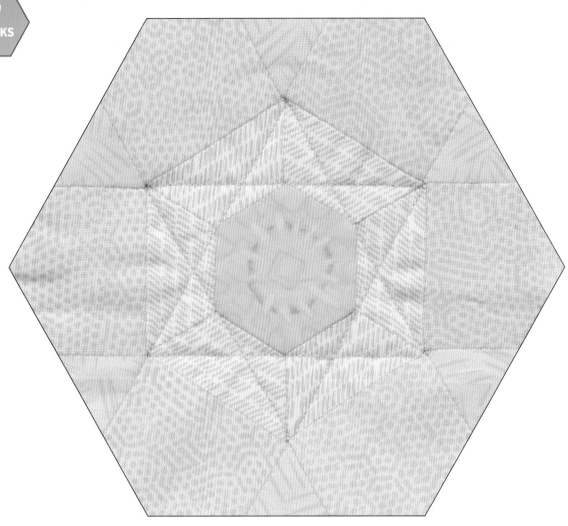

What to Cut

- 1 of A2
- 6 *each* of C1, F4, and Q3

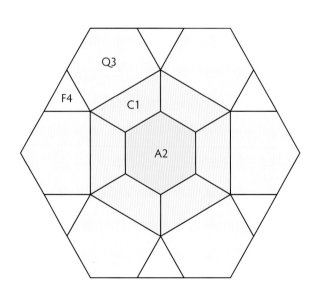

Bo-rayanne

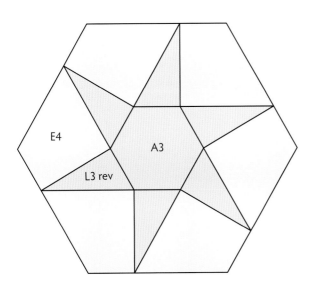

What to Cut

- 1 of A3
- 6 *each* of E4 and
  L3 reversed

Anne

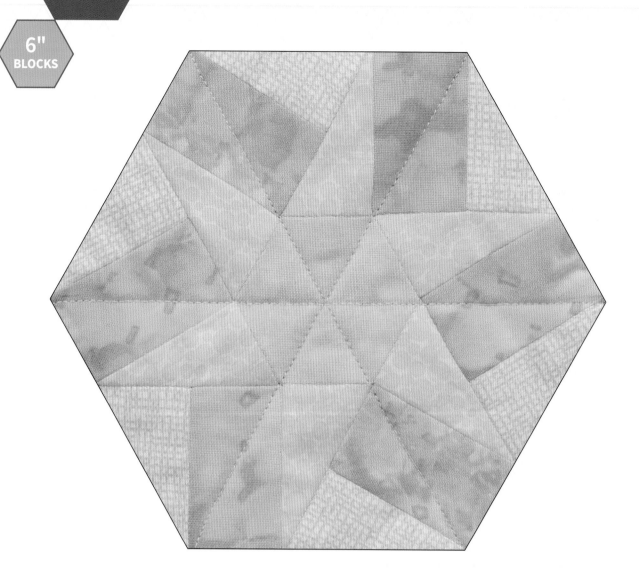

What to Cut

- 1 of A3
- 6 *each* of L3, L3 reversed, and M3

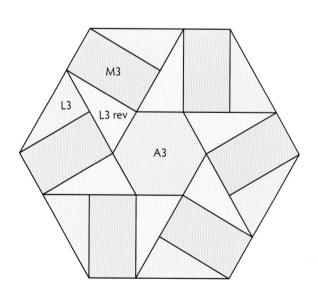

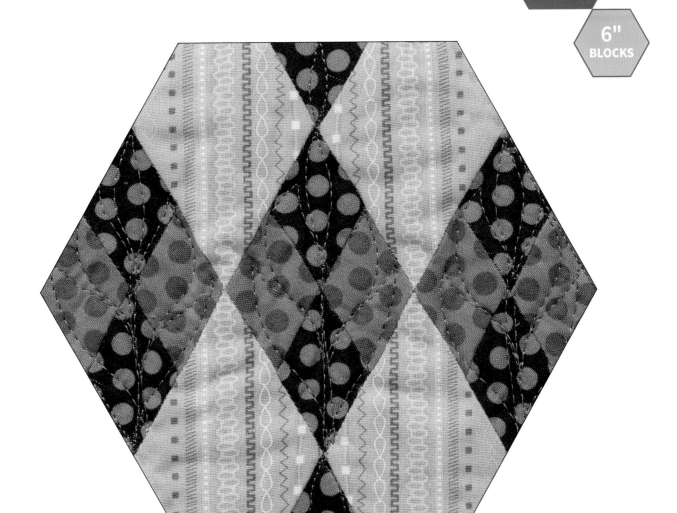

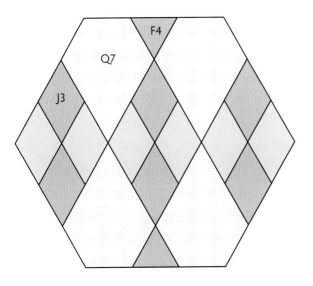

What to Cut

- 2 of F4
- 4 of Q7
- 12 of J3

BLOCK 30 Krista

6" BLOCKS

BLOCK
30 Krista

6" BLOCKS

What to Cut

- 6 *each* of J5 and P2
- 12 of K9

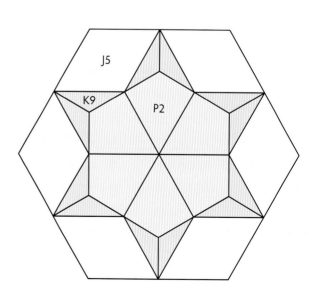

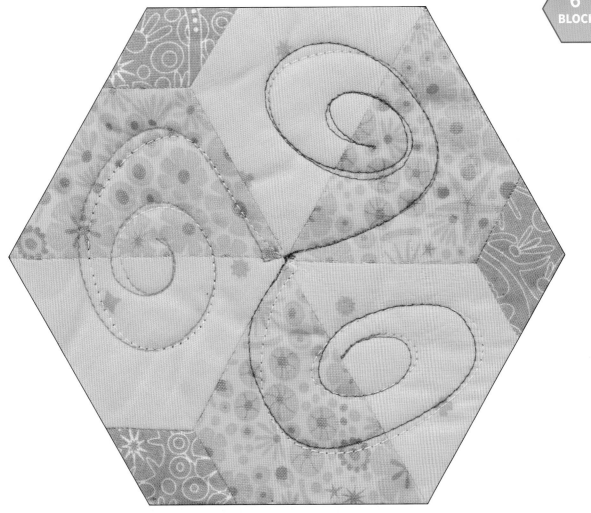

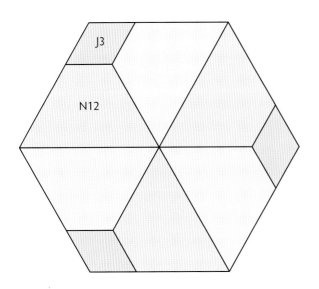

What to Cut

- 3 of J3
- 6 of N12

Gesine

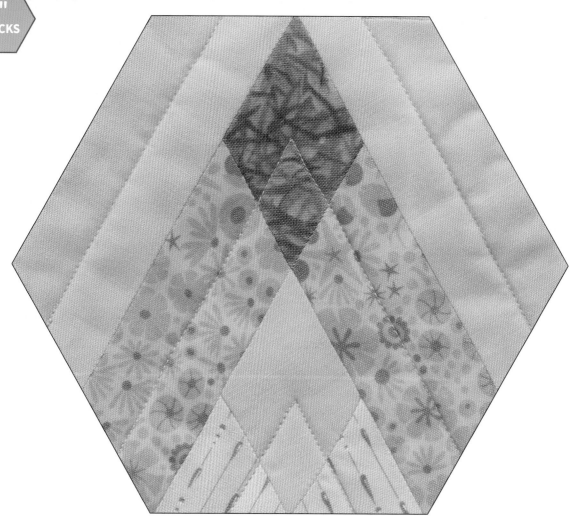

What to Cut

- 1 *each* of N4 and N4 reversed
- 2 *each* of F6, J5, and N14

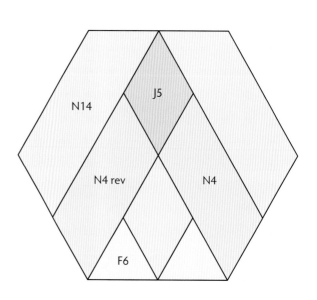

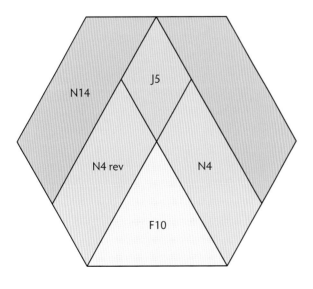

What to Cut

- 1 *each* of F10, J5, N4, and N4 reversed
- 2 of N14

Hayley

What to Cut

- 1 of A3
- 12 *each* of C2 and F4

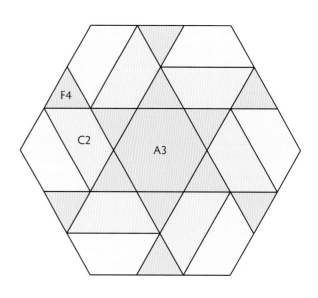

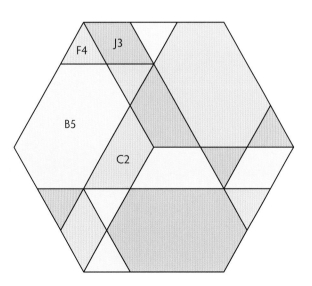

What to Cut

- 3 *each* of B5, C2, and J3
- 9 of F4

Heather

What to Cut

- 1 of A4
- 6 of F6
- 12 *each* of L2 and
  L2 reversed

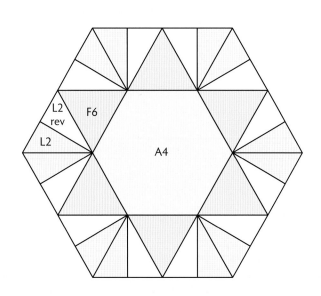

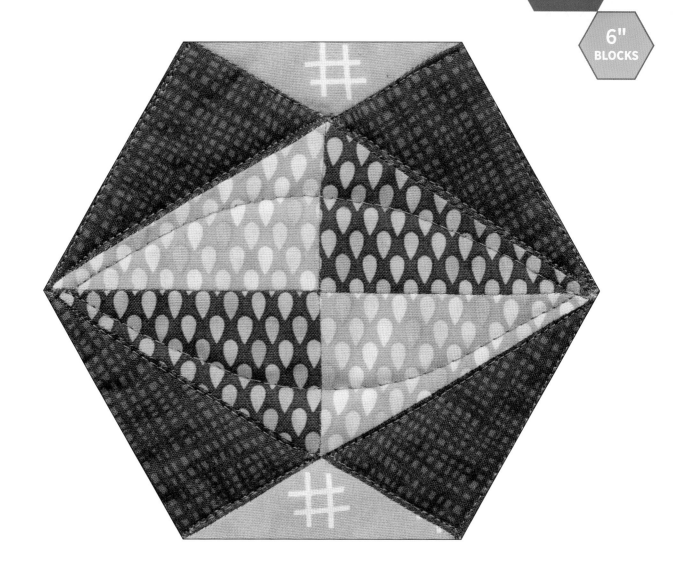

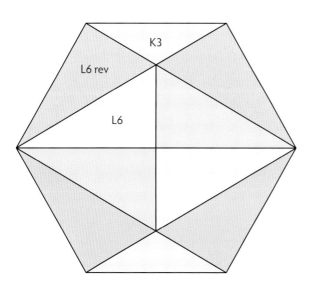

What to Cut

- 2 of K3
- 4 *each* of L6 and L6 reversed

Kathleen

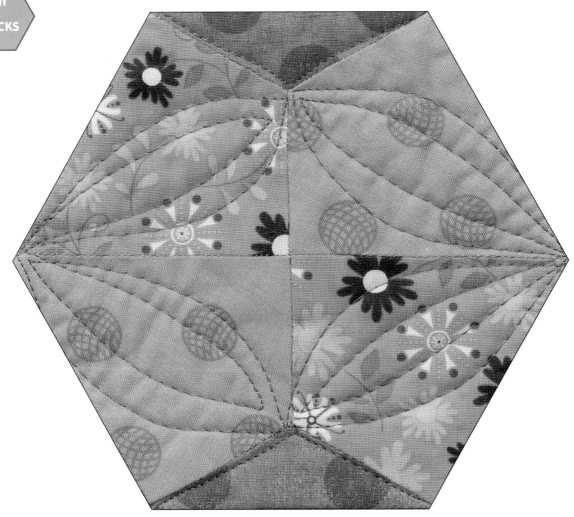

What to Cut

- 2 of K3
- 4 of P5

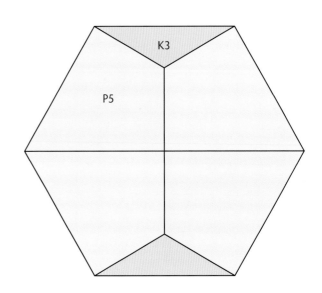

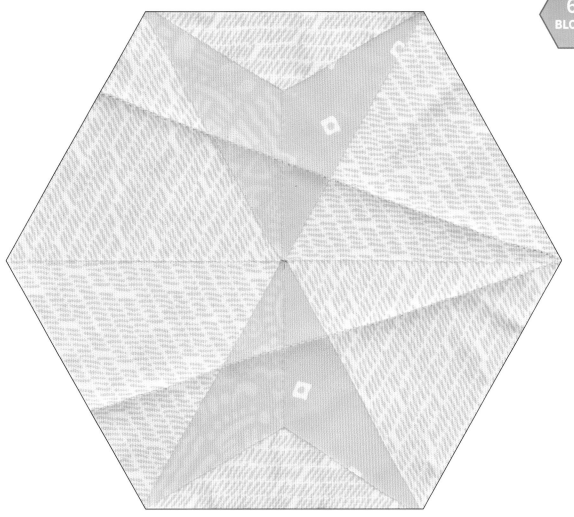

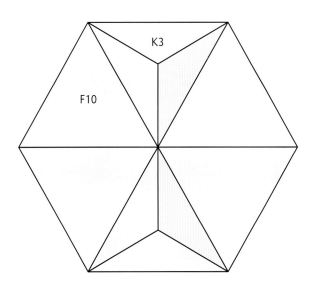

What to Cut

- 4 of F10
- 6 of K3

Maike

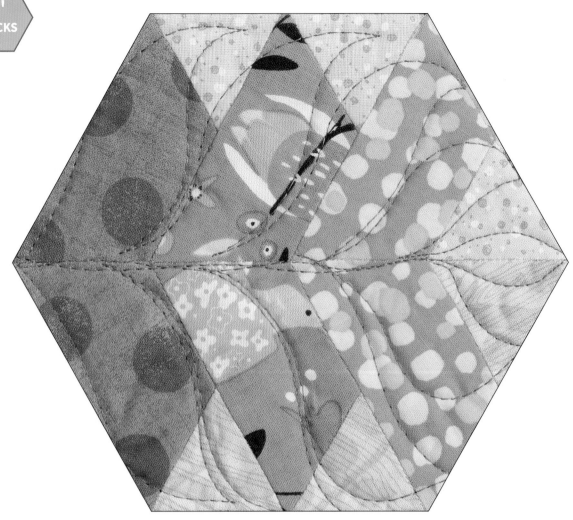

What to Cut

- 6 *each* of C3 and F6

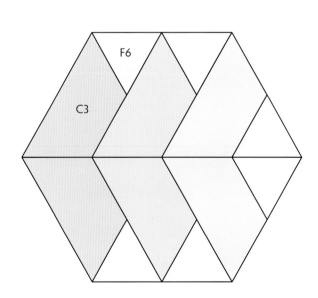

Ashley

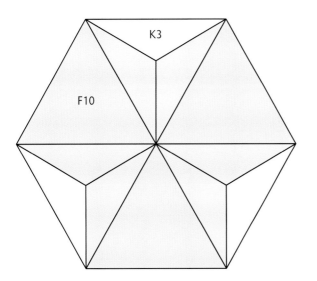

What to Cut

- 3 of F10
- 9 of K3

Jody

6"
BLOCKS

What to Cut

- 2 *each* of F7, K3, L1, L1 reversed, and Q16
- 4 of J6

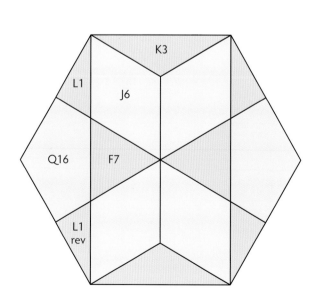

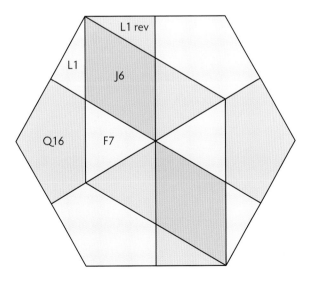

What to Cut

- 2 *each* of J6, L1, and L1 reversed
- 4 *each* of F7 and Q16

Christine

What to Cut

- 1 of J6
- 2 *each* of L1, L1 reversed, and P2
- 4 of F6
- 6 of J5

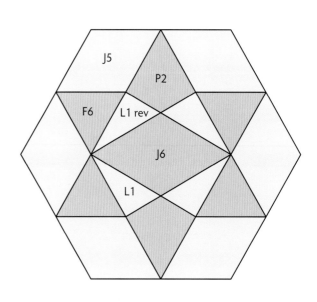

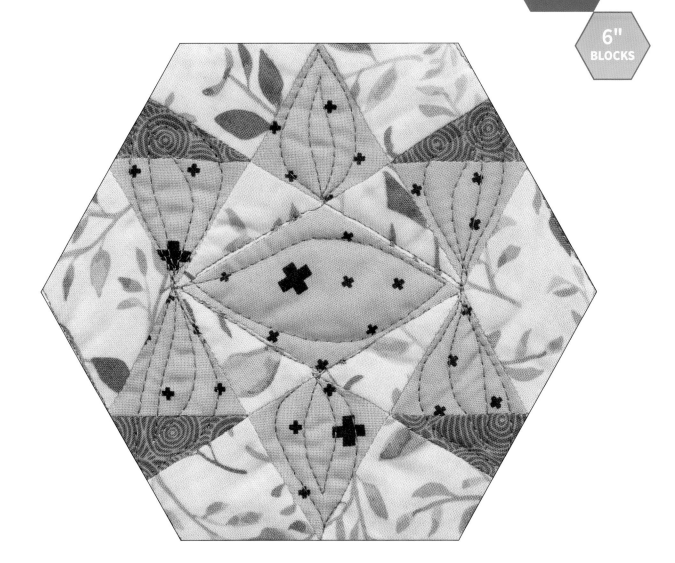

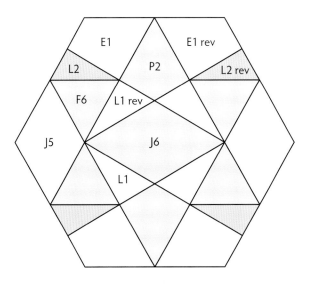

What to Cut

- 1 of J6
- 2 *each* of E1, E1 reversed, J5, L1, L1 reversed, L2, L2 reversed, and P2
- 4 of F6

Meg

What to Cut

- 6 *each* of J3 and Q7

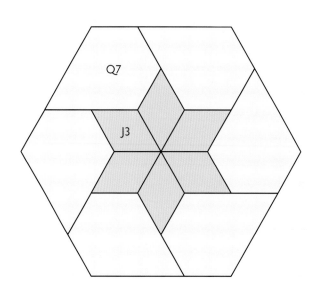

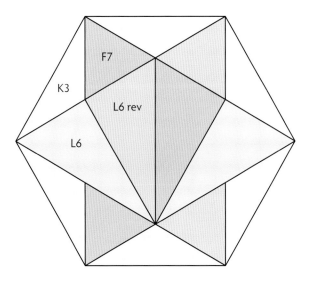

What to Cut

- 2 *each* of L6 and L6 reversed
- 4 of F7
- 6 of K3

Tonya

What to Cut

- 1 of F10
- 3 of K3
- 6 of Q16

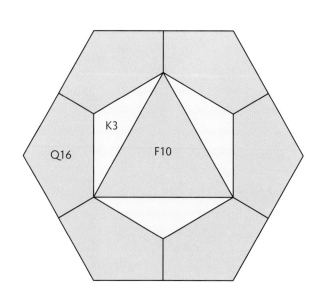

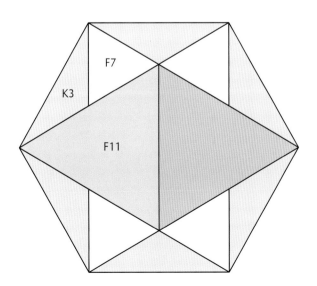

What to Cut

- 2 of F11
- 4 of F7
- 6 of K3

Alexandra

What to Cut

- 1 of F13
- 3 of F6
- 6 of J5

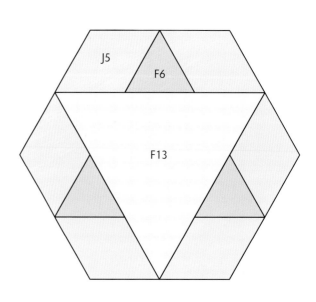

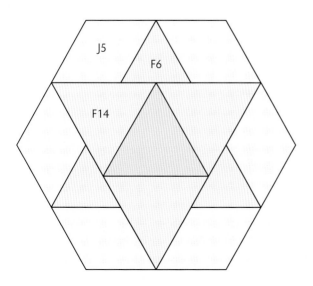

J5

F6

F14

What to Cut

- 3 of F6
- 4 of F14
- 6 of J5

Sabine

What to Cut

- 6 *each* of L5 and
  L5 reversed

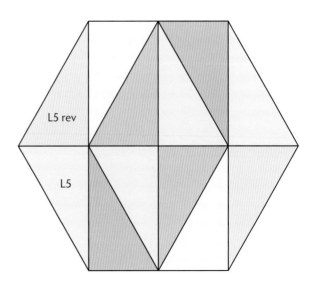

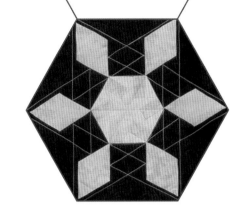

Explore the Stars
Bed Quilt

Finished quilt: 92" × 92"
(Queen size, no pillow tuck)

Blocks used:
- 4 assorted 12" blocks
- 20 assorted 6" blocks
- 18 assorted 2" equilateral triangles
- 6 assorted 3" equilateral triangles
- 6 assorted 3" half hexagons
- 78 assorted 1¾" six-point diamonds
- 24 assorted 3" six-point diamonds

Materials

Yardage is based on 42"-wide fabric, except where noted.

4¼ yards *total* of assorted yellow and gold prints for blocks and setting pieces

5⅞ yards of 108"-wide navy print for background and backing*

⅔ yard of navy print for binding

100" × 100" piece of batting

Water-soluble fabric marker

6" × 24" acrylic ruler

*If using 42"-wide fabric, you'll need 16 yards of fabrics. You'll also need to cut and piece the background and backing to make the size of squares listed in "Cutting" on page 68.

Backing Fabrics

TIP

When I started quilting, we always had to piece the backing for a bed quilt. Finding a wide fabric, other than basic muslin, to back a queen- or king-size quilt was almost impossible. Slowly, wide backing fabrics began to emerge on the market, but I often found the quality to be less than desirable. However, today's options are plentiful, and much of the quality is unsurpassed. I'm still very choosy about what I use to back my quilts. I feel that the fabric on the back of the quilt must be as good as the fabric on the front. Thankfully, today there are plenty of options.

Cutting

From the navy print for background and backing, cut:
1 square, 92" × 92"
1 square, 100" × 100"

From the navy print for binding, cut:
10 strips, 2⅛" × 42"

Piecing

Refer to "Techniques for Perfect English Paper Piecing" on pages 8–12 for detailed instructions as needed.

1. Referring to the blocks on pages 15–66, choose four 12" blocks and 20 assorted 6" blocks. I used one each of blocks 4, 5, 8, 13, 16, 24, 26, 28, 30, 34, 36, and 51. I used six each of blocks 32 and 39. Make the required templates for each block using the patterns on pages 83–91. Cut the pieces from the assorted yellow and gold prints. Assemble each block.

2. Using either pattern R on page 91 or precut Paper Pieces 3" half hexagons as a guide, cut six matching half hexagons from the yellow or gold prints, adding ⅜" around each shape for seam allowance. Glue baste the half hexagons to the paper pieces.

3. Using either pattern S on page 91 or precut Paper Pieces 2" equilateral triangles as a guide, cut six matching triangles from the yellow or gold prints, adding ⅜" around each shape for seam allowance. Glue baste the triangles to the paper pieces.

4. Using either pattern T on page 92 or precut Paper Pieces 3" equilateral triangles as a guide, cut six matching triangles from the yellow or gold prints, adding ⅜" around each shape for seam allowance. Glue baste the triangles to the paper pieces.

5. Using either patterns S, V, and W on pages 91–93 or precut Paper Pieces 2" equilateral triangles, 1¾" six-point diamonds, and 3" six-point diamonds as a guide, cut 12 matching triangles, 78 assorted 1¾" six-point diamonds, and 24 assorted 3" six-point diamonds from the yellow or gold prints, adding ⅜" around each shape for seam allowance. Glue baste the triangles and diamonds to the paper pieces.

6. Sew a 2" triangle from step 3 to the center of each outer edge of block 4, aligning the triangles along the block's outer edge. Sew a 3" half hexagon from step 2 to each outer edge of block 13. Sew six of block 32 to the outer edges of block 51; sew a 3" triangle from step 4 to the outermost edge of each block 32.

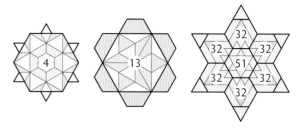

Make 1 of each.

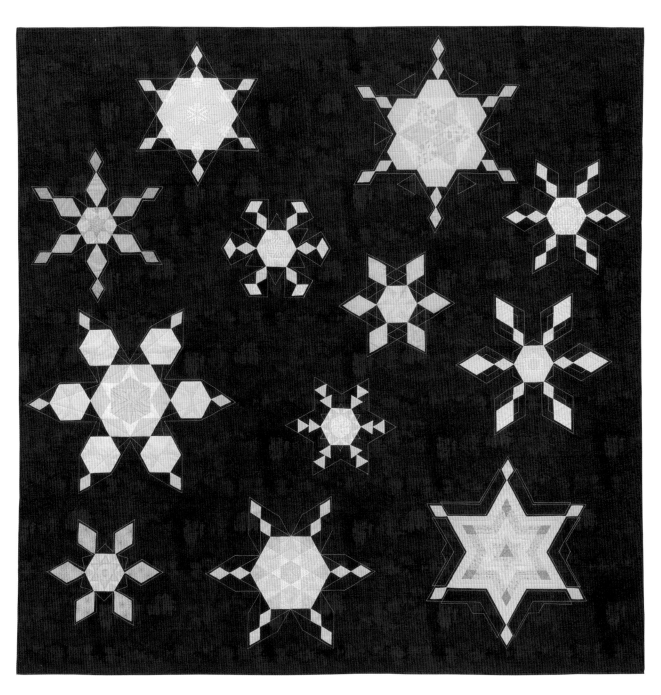

Explore the Stars
made by *Katja Marek*

Assembling the Quilt Top

1. Place the navy 92" square right side up on a large flat surface. Using a water-soluble fabric marker, place marks at the locations indicated in the diagram to mark the center point on the left side of each block.

2. Carefully press the blocks and setting pieces; then use a tailor's awl to remove the paper templates. Pin the blocks to the background in the locations shown, lining up the center point on the left side of each block with the marks. Appliqué the blocks in place.

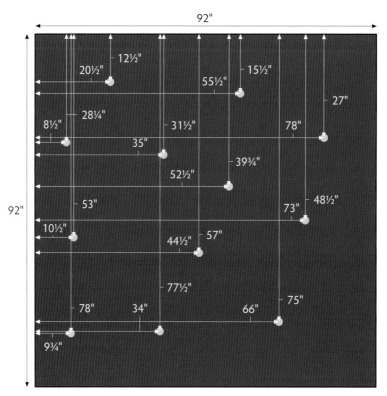

Placement diagram

3. Use a water-soluble fabric marker to draw a line extending outward from each corner of the block by lining up a 6" × 24" ruler with opposing corners on blocks 5, 8, 16, 24, 26, 28, 30, and 36. For blocks 4, 13, 34, and 51, draw a line bisecting the blocks through the center of two opposing sides.

4. Pin all of block 39 and the setting pieces (S, V, and W) to the background using the drawn lines as a guide to keep the angles accurate.

5. Appliqué the remaining blocks and setting pieces to the background to complete the quilt top. The quilt top should measure 92" square.

Quilt assembly

Finishing the Quilt

1. Layer the quilt top, batting, and backing; baste. Hand or machine quilt. I ruler quilted straight lines around and within each of the stars in yellow variegated thread, to enhance their sparkle. I then quilted navy swirls throughout the background between the stars.

2. Use the navy 2⅛"-wide strips to bind the quilt. For help with binding techniques, visit ShopMartingale.com/TheNewHexagon2.

Amethyst
Table Runner

Finished table runner: 26½" × 54½"

Blocks used:
- 4 assorted 12" blocks
- 6 assorted 6" blocks
- 178 assorted 3" equilateral triangles

Materials

Yardage is based on 42"-wide fabric.

2 yards *total* of assorted white prints for background

2 yards *total* of assorted purple, gray, and black prints for blocks

⅓ yard of gray print for binding

1¾ yards of fabric for backing

33" × 61" piece of batting

Cutting

From the gray print, cut:
4 strips, 2⅛" × 42"

Piecing

Refer to "Techniques for Perfect English Paper Piecing" on pages 8–12 for detailed instructions as needed.

1. Referring to the blocks on pages 15–66, choose four 12" blocks and six 6" blocks. I used two each of blocks 15–16, and six of block 23. Make the required

> Use your favorite fabrics and color combinations to display your English paper-piecing skills.

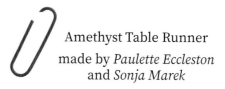

Amethyst Table Runner
made by *Paulette Eccleston*
and *Sonja Marek*

templates for each block using the patterns on pages 83–91. Cut the pieces from the assorted purple, gray, and black prints. Assemble each block.

2. Using either pattern T on page 92 or precut Paper Pieces 3" equilateral triangles as a guide, cut 178 triangles from the white prints, adding ⅜" around each shape for seam allowance. Glue baste the triangles to the paper pieces.

3. Hand stitch the blocks and background triangles together to make seven sections.

Make 7 sections.

4. Join the sections to complete the table runner.

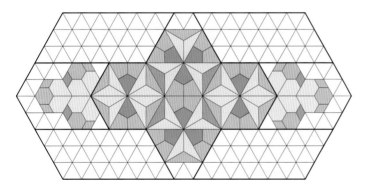

Table-runner assembly

5. Use a tailor's awl to remove the paper templates. Open all the seam allowances around the perimeter of the table-runner top and press.

Finishing the Table Runner

1. Layer the table-runner top, batting, and backing; baste. Hand or machine quilt. Paulette quilted a few simple straight lines through the blocks and background.

2. Use the gray 2⅛"-wide strips to bind the quilt. This quilt has 60° angles; if you need help with mitering the angles, you can visit ShopMartingale.com/TheNewHexagon2 for downloadable instructions.

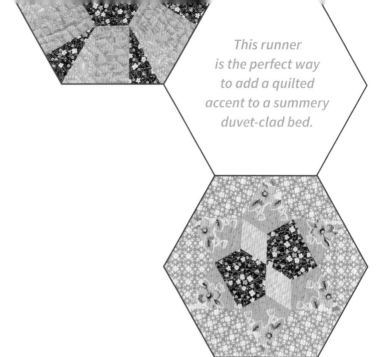

This runner is the perfect way to add a quilted accent to a summery duvet-clad bed.

Blossoms
Bed Runner

Finished bed runner: 84½" × 24½"

Blocks used:
- 3 assorted 12" blocks
- 4 assorted 6" blocks

Materials

Yardage is based on 42"-wide fabric.

1½ yards *total* of assorted pink, green, taupe, and black prints for blocks

2¼ yards *total* of cream prints for background

½ yard of taupe stripe for binding

2½ yards of fabric for backing

30" × 90" piece of batting

Cutting

From the cream prints, cut:
56 squares, 6½" × 6½"

From the taupe stripe, cut:
6 strips, 2⅛" × 42"

Assembling the Bed Runner

Refer to "Techniques for Perfect English Paper Piecing" on pages 8–12 for detailed instructions as needed. Press all seam allowances in the direction indicated by the arrows.

1. Referring to the blocks on pages 15–66, choose three assorted 12" blocks and four assorted 6" blocks. I used one of block 9, two of block 14, and four of block 25. Make the required templates for each block using the patterns on pages 83–91. Cut the pieces from the pink, green, taupe, and black prints. Assemble each block.

2. Arrange the cream squares in 14 rows of four squares each. Sew the squares together into rows. Join the rows to make the background section measuring 84½" × 24½", including seam allowances.

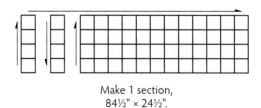

Make 1 section,
84½" × 24½".

Blossoms Bed Runner
made by *Bev Marcotte*

3. Press all the blocks and use a tailor's awl to remove the paper templates.

4. Arrange the blocks on the background section, aligning the points of the blocks with the seam intersections as shown. Appliqué the blocks in place.

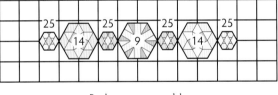

Bed-runner assembly

Finishing the Bed Runner

1. Layer the bed-runner top, batting, and backing; baste. Hand or machine quilt. Bev quilted random wavy lines across the length of the bed runner.

2. Use the taupe stripe 2⅛"-wide strips to bind the quilt. For help with binding techniques, visit ShopMartingale.com/TheNewHexagon2.

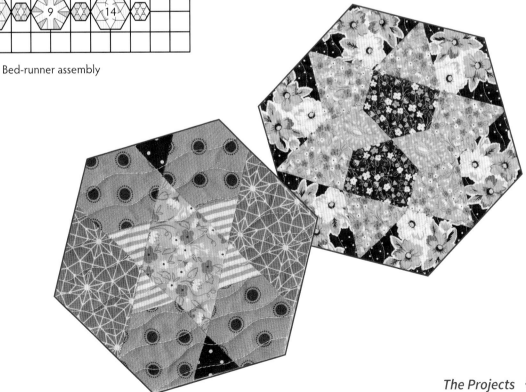

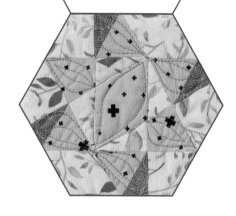

Argyle
Lap Quilt

Finished quilt: 48½" × 62⅞"

Blocks used:

- 7 assorted 12" blocks
- 6 assorted 12" half blocks
- 48 assorted 6" blocks
- 4 assorted 6" horizontal half blocks
- 8 assorted 6" vertical half blocks
- 20 assorted green 6" equilateral triangles
- 4 and 4 reversed assorted green 6" six-point quarter diamonds
- 100 assorted turquoise 3" equilateral triangles
- 8 and 8 reversed assorted turquoise 3" six-point quarter diamonds

Materials

Yardage is based on 42"-wide fabric.

4⅞ yards *total* of assorted turquoise prints for 6" blocks

3 yards *total* of assorted green prints for 12" blocks

1⅝ yards of turquoise tone on tone for setting triangles, quarter diamonds, and binding

⅝ yard of green tone on tone for setting triangles and quarter diamonds

3⅛ yards of fabric for backing

55" × 69" piece of batting

Cutting

From the green tone on tone, cut:

3 strips, 6½" × 42"

From the turquoise tone on tone, cut:

7 strips, 4¾" × 42"

1 strip, 3½" × 42"

6 strips, 2⅛" × 42"

Piecing

Refer to "Techniques for Perfect English Paper Piecing" on pages 8–12 for detailed instructions as needed.

1. Referring to the blocks on pages 15–66, choose 13 assorted 12" blocks and 60 assorted 6" blocks. I used one each of blocks 1, 4, 5, 6, 7, 13, and 14. I used two blocks each of 2, 8, and 11 to make half blocks. These blocks have a natural division in the center and the templates for one block can be used to piece each of the two halves. I used two each of blocks 15, 17, 20, 21, 22, 26, 27, 28, 29, 35, 37, 40, 41, 42, 43, 44, 45, 46, 47, 48, 49, and 50. I used one each of blocks 33, 38, 39, and 52. I used two each of blocks 38 and 52 to make horizontal half blocks. Again, these blocks have a natural division in the center. I used two each of blocks 18, 33, 39, and 52 to make vertical half blocks. Block 52 has a natural division in the center. However, for blocks 18, 33, and 39 one or more of the template pieces may need to be cut in half in the center to

Argyle
made by *Linda King*

make two half blocks, or complete blocks can be made and trimmed after assembling the quilt top. Make the required templates for each block using the patterns on pages 83–91. Cut the pieces for the 12" blocks from the assorted green prints. Cut the pieces for the 6" blocks from the assorted turquoise prints. Assemble each block.

2. Using either patterns U and Z on pages 92 and 93 or precut Paper Pieces 6" equilateral triangles and 6" six-point quarter diamonds as a guide, cut 20 triangles from the green tone-on-tone strips, adding ⅜" around each shape for seam allowance. Cut four quarter diamonds and four reversed quarter diamonds from the assorted green strips, adding ⅜" around each shape for seam allowance. Glue baste the shapes to the paper pieces.

3. Using either pattern T on page 92 or precut Paper Pieces 3" equilateral triangles as a guide, cut 100 triangles from the turquoise tone-on-tone 4¾"-wide strips, adding ⅜" around each shape for seam allowance. Glue baste the triangles to the paper pieces.

4. Using either pattern Y on page 93 or precut Paper Pieces 3" six-point quarter diamonds as a guide, cut eight and eight reversed quarter diamonds from the turquoise tone-on-tone 3½" strip, adding ⅜" around each shape for seam allowance. Glue baste the quarter diamonds to the paper pieces.

5. Hand stitch green triangles to opposite sides of each 12" block to make seven block units. Hand stitch a green triangle to the top edge of each 12" half block to make six half-block units. Hand stitch a green quarter diamond to the short edge of each green reversed quarter diamond to make four side units.

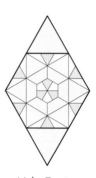

Make 7 units.

Make 6 units.   Make 4 units.

6. Hand stitch turquoise triangles to opposite sides of each 6" block to make 48 block units. Hand stitch a turquoise triangle to the top edge of each 6" horizontal half block to make four half-block units. Hand stitch a turquoise quarter diamond and a turquoise reversed quarter diamond to the top and bottom of each vertical half block to make eight side units.

Make 48 units.

Make 4 units.   Make 8 units.

7. Lay out the block units in diagonal rows. Add the half-block units to the top and bottom edges and place the side units along the side edges. Sew the blocks, half blocks, and side units together into diagonal rows. Join the rows to complete the quilt top.

8. Use a tailor's awl to remove the paper templates. Open all the seam allowances around the perimeter of the quilt top and press.

Finishing the Quilt

1. Layer the quilt top, batting, and backing; baste. Hand or machine quilt. Linda ruler quilted straight lines along the edges of most blocks and enhanced the insides of each block with random free-motion quilting. She repeated the same leafy design in each of the 3" and 6" triangles.

2. Use the turquoise 2⅛"-wide strips to bind the quilt. For help with binding techniques, visit ShopMartingale.com/TheNewHexagon2.

Quilt assembly

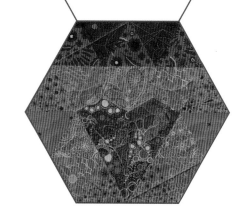

I love to find the possibilities in block combinations to make them flow and become extraordinary!

Starburst
Wall Quilt

Finished quilt: 52½" × 60½"

Blocks used:
- 13 assorted 12" blocks
- 30 assorted 6" blocks
- 60 assorted 3" equilateral triangles
- 24 assorted 3" six-point diamonds

Materials

Yardage is based on 42"-wide fabric.

7⅝ yards *total* of assorted yellow, blue, purple, pink, and coral prints for blocks

⅓ yard of pink print for binding

3⅓ yards of fabric for backing

59" × 67" piece of batting

Cutting

From the pink print, cut:

5 strips, 2⅛" × 42"

Piecing

Refer to "Techniques for Perfect English Paper Piecing" on pages 8–12 for detailed instructions as needed.

1. Referring to the blocks on pages 15–66, choose 13 assorted 12" blocks and 30 assorted 6" blocks. I used one of blocks 8 and 12 of block 19. I used six each of blocks 10, 14, 18, 31, and 33. Make the required templates for each block using the patterns on pages 83–91. Cut the pieces from the yellow, blue, purple, pink, and coral prints. Assemble each block.

2. Using either pattern T on page 92 or precut Paper Pieces 3" equilateral triangles as a guide, cut 30 triangles from the yellow prints, 6 triangles from the pink prints, and 24 triangles from the coral prints, adding ⅜" around each shape for seam allowance. Glue baste the triangles to the paper pieces.

3. Using either pattern W on page 93 or precut Paper Pieces 3" six-point diamonds as a guide, cut 24 diamonds from the purple prints, adding ⅜" around each shape for seam allowance. Glue baste the diamonds to the paper pieces.

4. Using a whipstitch, join three yellow triangles. Make six units.

Make 3 of each unit.

Starburst

made by *Sonja Marek* and *Katja Marek*

5. Attach the units to the edges of block 8 to make the center block.

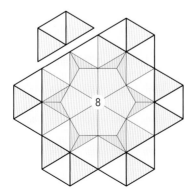

6. Hand stitch blocks 18 and 33 around the center block, alternating them as shown. Sew a pink 3" triangle to the top of each block 33.

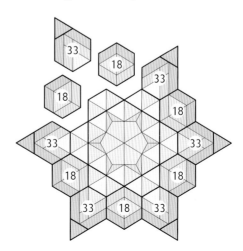

7. Use a whipstitch to join two diamonds. Make six units that slant to the left and six units that slant to the right.

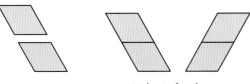

Make 6 of each unit.

8. Hand stitch the diamond units from step 7 to blocks 18 and 33. Attach blocks 10 and 14 around the perimeter, alternating them as shown.

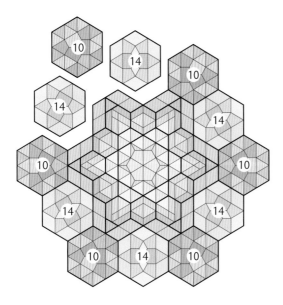

9. Hand stitch yellow triangles to opposite sides of each block 31 to make six units. Hand stitch coral triangles to opposite sides of each block 19 to make 12 units.

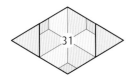

Make 6 units.

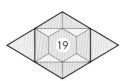

Make 12 units.

10. Hand stitch one block 31 unit and two block 19 units together. Make six.

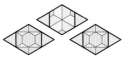 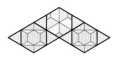

Make 6 units.

11. Hand stitch the units from step 10 to the quilt-top center to complete the quilt top.

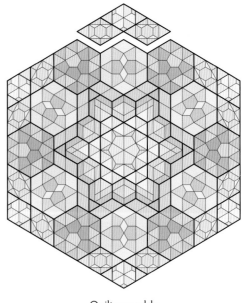

Quilt assembly

12. Open all the seam allowances around the perimeter and carefully press the quilt top. Use a tailor's awl to remove the paper templates.

Finishing the Quilt

1. Layer the quilt top, batting, and backing; baste. Hand or machine quilt. I quilted a combination of straight lines, swirls, and feathers throughout, including straight lines in the center star for emphasis.

2. Use the pink 2⅛"-wide strips to bind the quilt. For help with mitering the angles, visit ShopMartingale.com/TheNewHexagon2 for downloadable instructions.

Pattern Pieces

For the blocks in *The New Hexagon,* I didn't think beyond those first 52 blocks when it came to sorting the individual shapes. However, when I designed the blocks for *The New Hexagon Perpetual Calendar,* I soon realized there would be a lot of pieces to keep track of. So, I sorted the patterns into groups that made sense to me. I've used those pattern designations again for the blocks in this book. If a pattern already exists in *The New Hexagon Perpetual Calendar,* it will have the same letter/number designation in this book. If the pattern is a new size, it will be sorted into the same group based on its shape and assigned a new sequential number.

The patterns are sorted into the following groups:

Used for blocks:

- A: Hexagons
- B: Irregular hexagons and cupcakes
- C: Half hexagons
- D: One-third hexagons
- E: One-quarter hexagons
- F: Equilateral triangles
- G: Isosceles triangles
- H: Miscellaneous triangles
- J: Six-point diamonds
- K: Six-point half diamonds
- L: Six-point quarter diamonds
- M: Squares and rectangles
- N: Parallelograms, tumblers, and trapezoids
- O: Quadrilaterals
- P: Chrysanthemums and kites
- Q: Irregular pentagons, houses, and jewels

Used for settings:

- R: Half hexagon
- S: Equilateral triangle
- T: Equilateral triangle
- U: Equilateral triangle
- V: Six-point diamond
- W: Six-point diamond
- X: Six-point half diamond
- Y: Six-point quarter diamond
- Z: Six-point quarter diamond

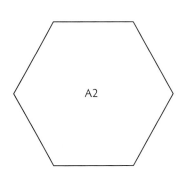

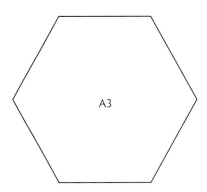

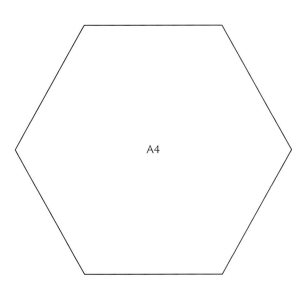

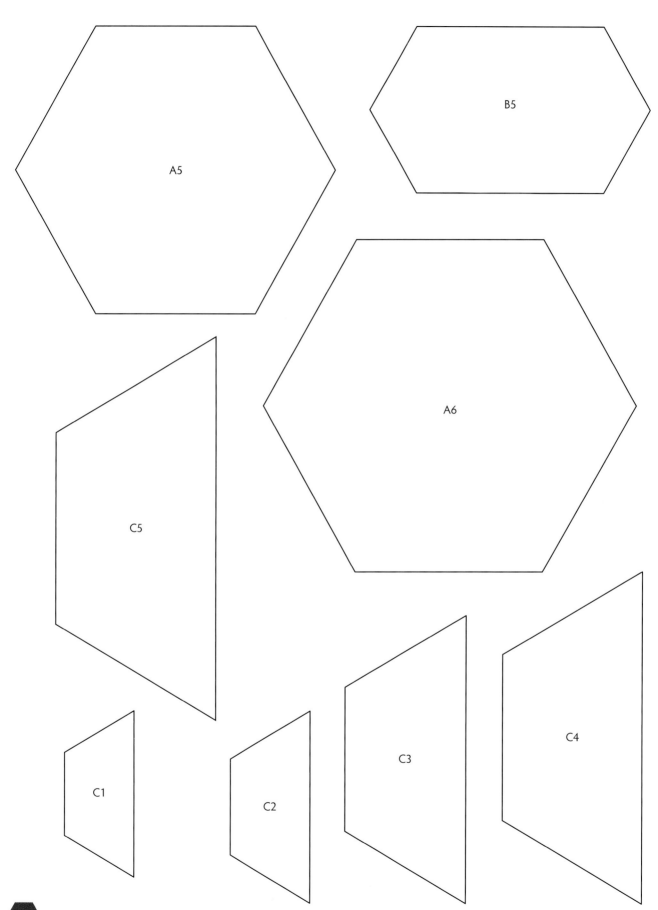

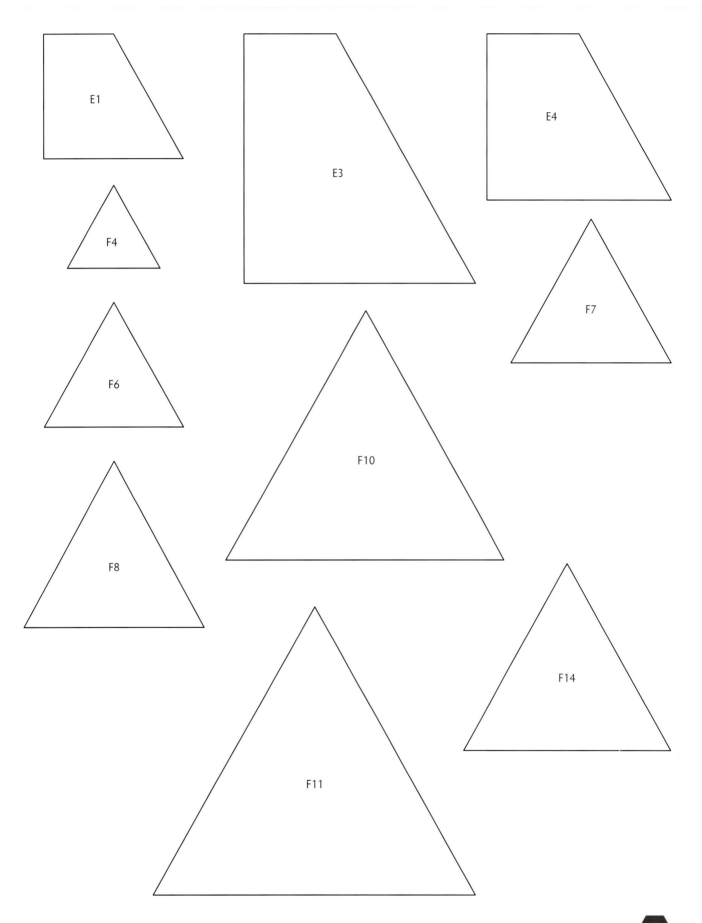

E1

F4

E3

E4

F7

F6

F10

F8

F11

F14

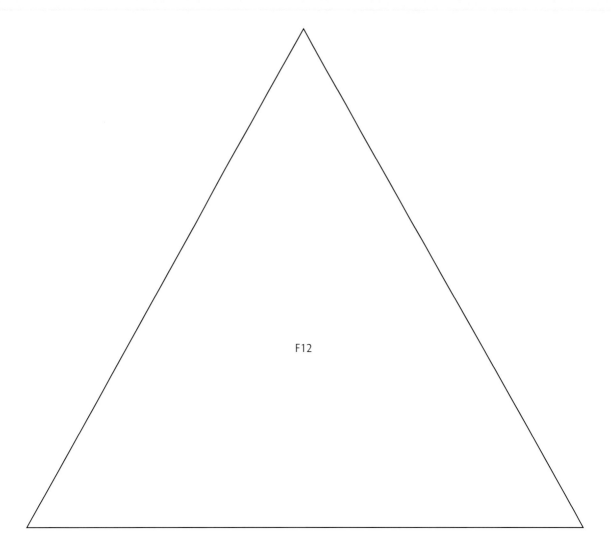

F12

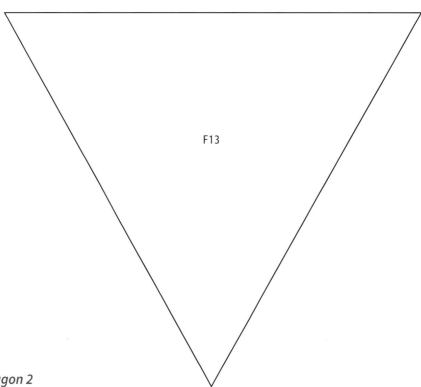

F13

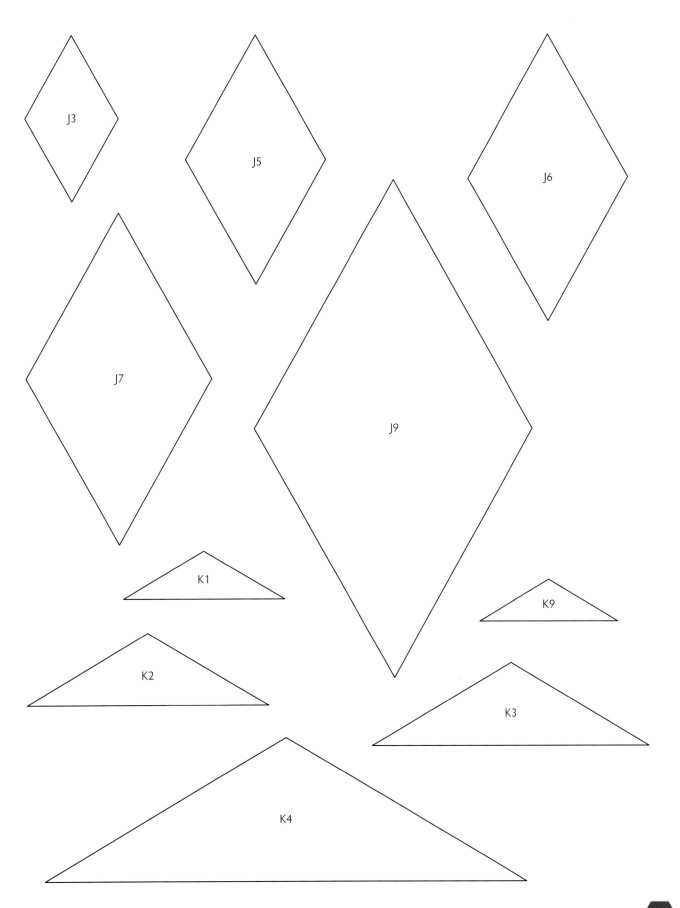

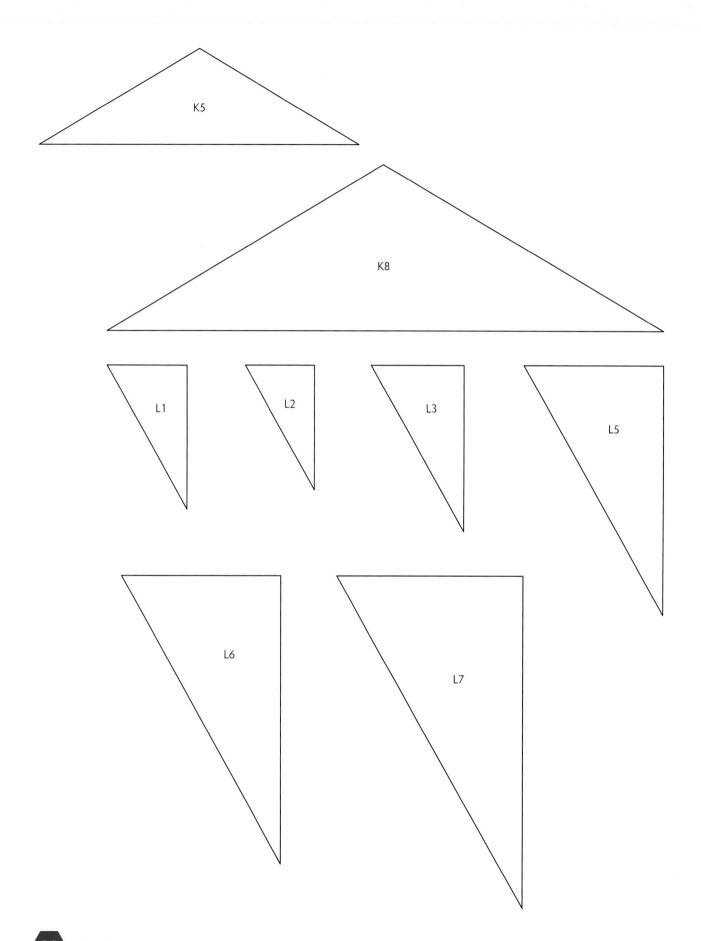

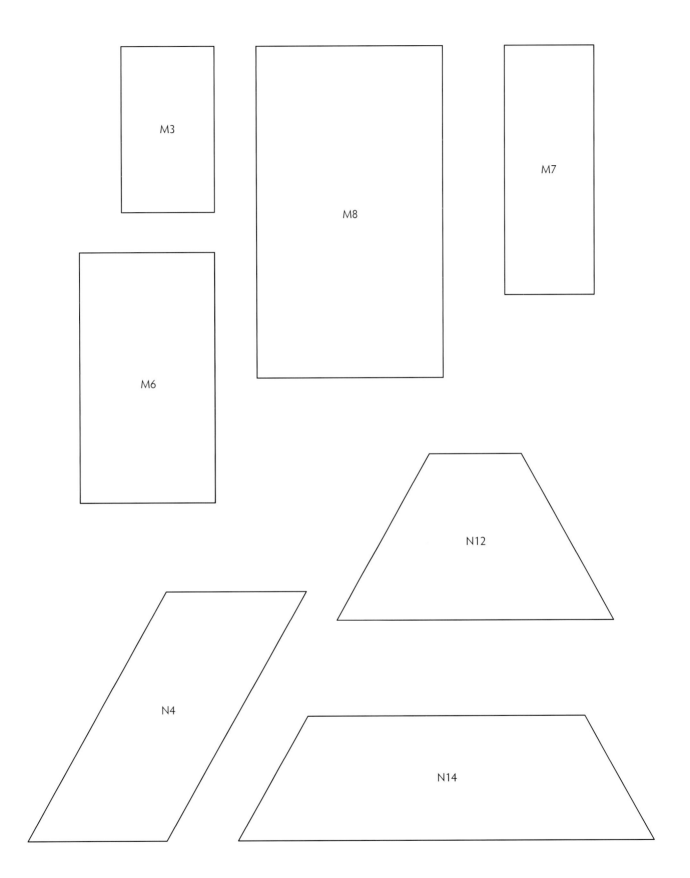

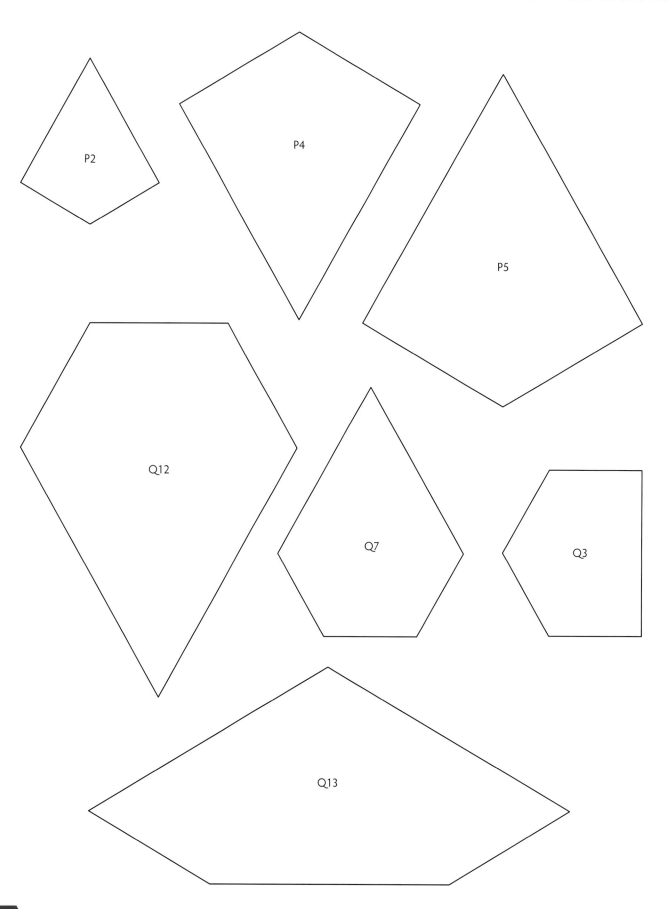

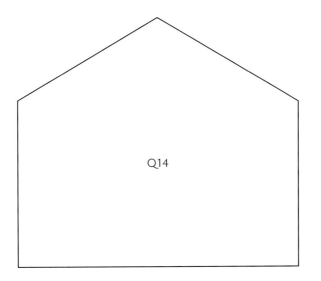

Q14

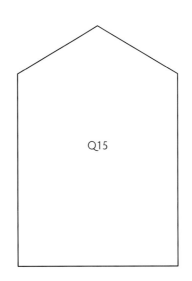

Q15

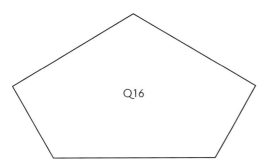

Q16

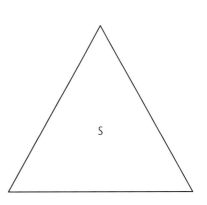

S

Setting Patterns

Although many of these pieces also exist within the block patterns, they serve a different function when used for setting the blocks. The patterns are shown here for easy access.

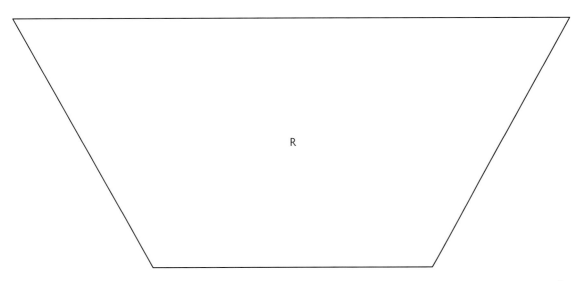

R

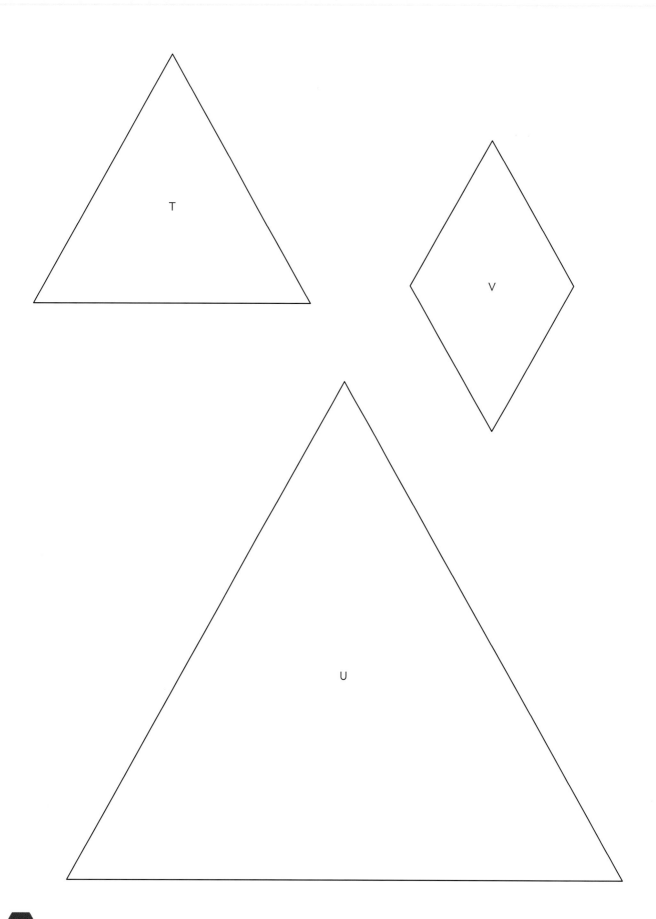

T

V

U

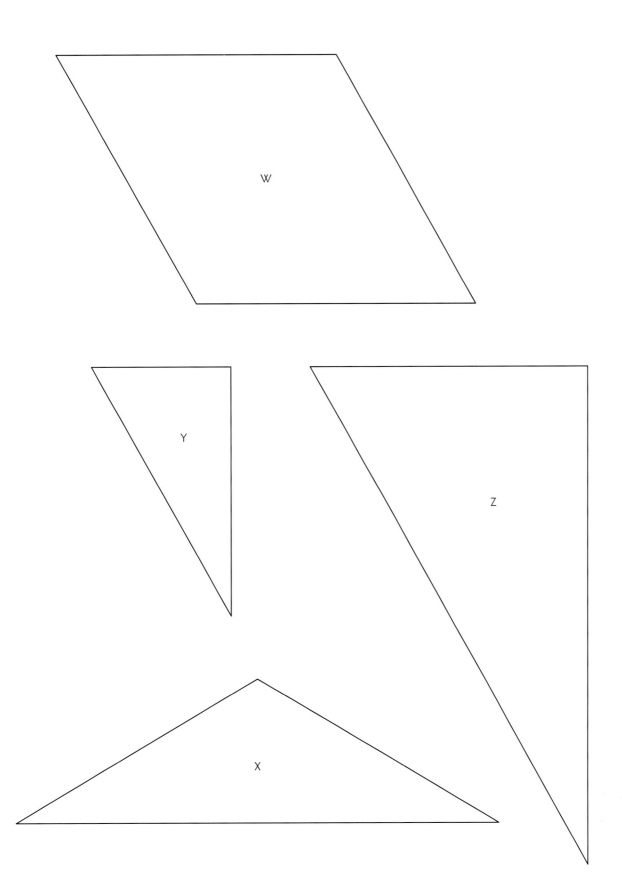

Resources

Many of the supplies referred to throughout this book are available at your local quilt shop. If you can't find them in your area, try these websites.

Aurifil
Aurifil.com
50-weight 100% cotton thread

CM Designs
AddAQuarter.com
Add-Three-Eighths ruler

Clover
Clover-usa.com
Appliqué pins, marking pens, needles, needle threader, and Hera marker

Collins
Prym-Consumer-usa.com
Fine line water erasable marking pen and water-soluble glue stick and refills

Hobbs Batting
HobbsBondedFibers.com
Thermore 100% polyester batting

Katja's Quilt Shoppe
KatjasQuiltShoppe.com
General quilting supplies and fabric

Mettler
Amann-Mettler.com
Silk-finish 50-weight 100% cotton thread

Odif USA
Odifusa.com
Temporary fabric adhesives

Paper Pieces
PaperPieces.com
Precut paper packs for English paper piecing and precision laser-cut acrylics

Superior Threads
SuperiorThreads.com
50-weight 100% cotton thread

WonderFil
WonderFil.ca
InvisaFil 100-weight 2-ply cottonized polyester thread

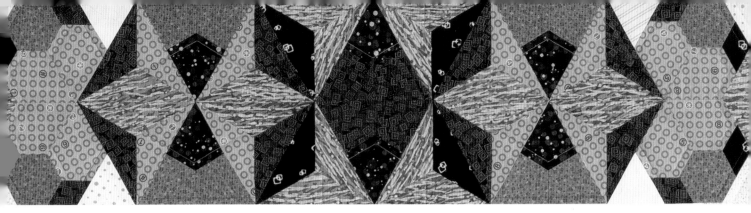

Acknowledgments

A heartfelt thank-you to all of the following:

Paper Pieces, who agreed to work with me to create the papers for every book, calendar, and quilt-along I've come up with, and now again for this book!

Paulette Eccleston, Nicole Gendy, Linda King, Bev Marcotte, and my mom, Sonja Marek, who helped by working on samples for this book. I wouldn't have been able to get it all done on time by myself. I so appreciate every one of you!

All my customers, who have given me the most enjoyable years of my life by allowing me to do what I love best.

Nancy Mahoney, who takes my words and makes them cohesive in a way I could never do on my own.

Moda Fabrics, who sent me some of the fabrics used in the projects for this book.

Martingale, I will forever be grateful for that first yes, and every one after.

Quilt-Along Facts

Downloads for all Katja Marek Quilt-Alongs can be found at KatjasQuiltShoppe.com under the Quilt-Alongs tab. The Facebook group for these and any future Quilt-Alongs is Katja Marek's "Quilt With Me" and can be found at: www.facebook.com/groups/534929129996575/

A New Quilt-Along based on blocks from this book, *The New Hexagon 2,* launches January 2020.

The New Hexagon - Millefiore Quilt-Along is based on *The New Hexagon: 52 Blocks to English Paper Piece.* (Join the Facebook group for this quilt-along at: www.facebook.com/groups/NewHexMillefiore/)

Blocks on the Go, for Quilts on the Grow, and **Hex-plosion** are based on *The New Hexagon: 52 Blocks to English Paper Piece.*

Perpetually Hexie is based on *The New Hexagon Perpetual Calendar.*

Rainy Days and Sun Days is based on *Distinctive Dresdens: 26 Intriguing Blocks, 6 Projects.*

Millie Stars is based on a combination of blocks from *The New Hexagon: 52 Blocks to English Paper Piece* and *The New Hexagon Perpetual Calendar.*

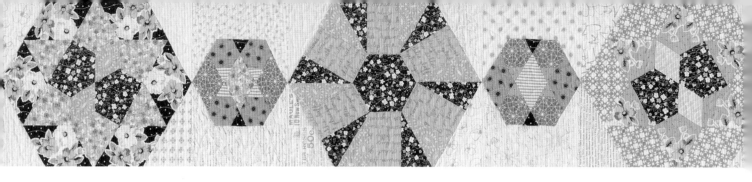

About the Author

Katja was born in Moers, Germany. When she was eight years old, her family immigrated to Canada. Her mother was a tailor by trade and, in order to stay home with her children, took in alterations. Katja grew up under her mother's sewing machine and spent many childhood hours crafting, sewing, crocheting, and cross-stitching. Unlike most young girls, as a teenager, Katja spent her money not on makeup and music but on fabric. When she was 14, Katja's family moved to a camp/resort, where many of the cabin beds had handmade quilts on them. She fell in love with an old version of a Grandmother's Fan design. Without any knowledge of quilting, but with a vast knowledge of sewing, she proceeded to make templates and cut pieces from old clothing. Thus her quilting journey had begun. When she won the award for art achievement in high school, she realized that she wanted to pursue a career with a creative outlet. In 1999, with years of banking behind her and her children in their teens, the time had come to realize that dream. She opened a quilt shop in x, British Columbia, Canada, which was featured in the Fall 2008 *Quilt Sampler* magazine.

Katja is also the author of *The New Hexagon: 52 Blocks to English Paper Piece* (Martingale, 2014), which was the #1 selling title for Martingale in 2015; *The New Hexagon Perpetual Calendar* (Martingale, 2016); *The New Hexagon Coloring Book* (Martingale, 2016); and *Distinctive Dresdens: 26 Intriguing Blocks, 6 Projects* (Martingale, 2017). She is the designer of several highly successful online quilt-alongs: The New Hexagon – Millefiore Quilt-Along; Blocks on the Go, for Quilts on the Grow; Perpetually Hexie; Hex-plosion; Rainy Days and Sun Days; and Millie Stars.